MW00881529

Great Pyrenees

Owner's Handbook

By Joseph B. Gentzel

Published by

Pyrenean Journal

an imprint of

Your Pet Place Administration, Inc.

29 Galilee Church Road

Jefferson, GA 30549

yourpetplace@windstream.net

About the Author

Maryann and I were married in 1964. Maryann worked while I went to college. I graduated with High Honors from the University of Florida with a BS in Physical Therapy in 1968 and was elected to the scholastic honor society of Phi Kappa Phi. I subsequently pursued postgraduate study that included Johns Hopkins, Emory University, and University of North Carolina that led to specializations in Electrophysiology and Applied Kinesology. I practiced Physical Therapy in independent practice until 1998. I maintain my certification as a Registered Physical Therapist currently. We have six children and at present have three grandchildren.

Maryann and I became acquainted with Great Pyrenees in 1972 when Maryann's mother was moving from a house to an apartment and could not take her Great Pyrenees, "Snowy".

That began an association and love affair with the Great Pyrenees that has lasted the best part of a lifetime. An association that has, over the years, involved our whole family of six children.

Today, many in the family are involved in dogs. We manage a large boarding kennel. Our youngest son, Gaelen is a professional dog handler who exhibits at over 100 dog shows per year.

We were the first Great Pyrenees breeders to remain active over this long period of time in the southeastern United States We have seen the coyote move into the region along with explosion of goats and some other pasture livestock flourish in the southeast. The result has been a growing demand for Great Pyrenees. I have placed and consulted with farmers in over70 different situations relative to the working Great Pyrenees. We are not farmers, but our working so closely with so many over such a long period of time has given us the knowledge to know the needs and circumstances of the working Great Pyrenees. I understand the breed's function historically and what is occurring in our contemporary society relative the breed.

Joe and Maryann with a young Pyr, Andre, taken in March 2008

We have bred many Great Pyrenees litters over the years. We have either bred or owned approximately 100 Pyrs that have finished their AKC championship. We have shown dogs to Best In Show and have dogs in both the show and top producers Hall of Fame of the Great Pyrenees Club of America. We have traveled

3

to France and England over 20 times in our study and education of the breed.

I am finishing up six years on the Board of Directors of the Great Pyrenees Club of American, Inc. as this is being written in March 2008. I have written many articles for publications, including the AKC Gazette, Bulletin of the Great Pyrenees Club of America, the English club magazine, the French club magazine, and others. I have consulted with the University of Georgia College of Veterinary Medicine in the area of wound healing and physical rehabilitation. In 2002, I wrote and published a book on the breed, *The Great Pyrenees: From France With Love.* I have written the history of the breed in several forms including the breed descriptions used by the American Kennel Club. I have been featured in the Gazette of the American Kennel Club. I have just finished writing *Roi-- Shepherd King's Dog*, a fiction novel where the main character, Roi, is a Great Pyrenees.

This Owners Handbook is for all owners, especially new or prospective owners. It also addresses, in a special section, the Great Pyrenees as livestock guardian dogs.

Table of Contents

History

Monsieur Theodore Dretzen on left with Champion Porthos and Madam Dretzen on right at a Paris dog show circa 1911. Porthos was proclaimed the most beautiful dog in France that year.

The Great Pyrenees is a very ancient breed. It becomes an academic question on just how ancient and why is it important? It is important because of the ancestral relationship, if any, between the Pyr and the other livestock guardian dogs (LGD). Some of these LGD are likely ancestors to the Pyr.

The question becomes, when did the Pyr become the breed we know from the Pyrenees Mountains, and what dogs, if any, preceded it? These questions are always linked to where did the

Pyr come from, or did it originate in the Pyrenees Mountains naturally from dogs indigenous to the region? There is disagreement over almost every point. There have been several theories advanced.

In my book published in 2002, The Great Pyrenees; From France With Love, I have an extensive bibliography and have footnoted current relevant study and thought in this area.

Dr. András Kovács outlines the case very well. "On the basis of archeological, geographical, cytogentic (sheep) and morphological evidences it can be stated that the flock guardians of Eurasia are from the same stock, but their origin is not Tibet, but the area of today's Kurdistan. It may be supposed too, that the

Kurdish sheep guarding dog- living in the area of its origin- is the common ancestor of others,

Akbash bitch and her puppy. A Great Pyrenees ancestor?

including the Tibetan Mastiff. It also means that the group of flock guards is probably at least 11,000 years old, existing long before written history. The earliest evidence of domestic sheep is from 9000 B.C." Dr. Kovács and many others make the case for these very early dogs that found favor with mankind in its need to provide protection for its flocks. These dogs, he termed the Kurdish Sheep Guarding dogs, are the ancestors of all the LGD's. He further delineates the evolution of two distinct types of large dogs that seem to co exist in the same geographical regions over time and location and the Kurdish Sheep Guarding dog is the ancestor to them both.

What we see is the more refined "lighter brighter" dogs that are termed lupomossoloids, and the heavier true mastiff dogs that he refers to as "heavier darker dogs." The "lighter brighter dogs" were mostly used for flock guarding. The "heavier darker dogs" were mostly used to guard property and homes. One can imagine

how, over eleven thousand years, these two distinct types could be intermingled and many times lost their distinctive types, but the two still exist enough, even today, that it

Monsieur Théodore Dretzen shown with

Champion Porthos in 1911

can be clearly seen.

The current day Pyr, Kuvasz, Tatra Mountain dog, Akbash dog, Slovakian Chuvatch, Maremma Sheepdog, Tornjac, and many others represent the "lighter brighter dogs". These dogs are all principally white, lupomossoloid phenotype flock guardian dogs historically. We see them mostly in the mountains. There are many other lesser-known representatives of this group and others that are extinct over the ages. The Kangal dog, St. Bernard, Pyrenean Mastiff, Spanish Mastiff, Tibetan Mastiff, Komondor, Sarplaninac, and many others represent the "heavier darker dogs". The purity of these delineations have long been lost and it is pretty muddy, or impossible today to make some of these delineations, but enough exist to see the difference. These "heavier darker dogs" are generally heavier, more bone, have true mastiff heads and bodies, they tend to have dark masks, and many times are dun colored with the coat being short. You can see there is a remarkable difference between the two types, as described above and outlined very nicely by Dr Kovács and those who concur with his study.

Le Marché aux Chiens circa 1907

One of the things we must acknowledge and keep in our minds as we review the literature, is that there were and still are at least two breeds and possibly a third in the same general region that have been confused

12

with one another. The region I refer is the Pyrenees Mountains, both the Spanish and French sides. Potentially two other breeds could have been mistaken for the Pyr over time in the region of the Pyrenees Mountains. In addition to the Pyr, we see the Pyrenean Mastiff and the Spanish Mastiff, both classic mastiff types. The Pyr is a lupomolossoid, but it is easy to see how the observer could confuse these dogs, especially those with little actual knowledge and experience of the breeds. We see many instances throughout the literature where one has to wonder if the writer is reporting a

Pyr, one of these other breeds, or some crossbred specimen. Additionally, to add to the confusion, the

Two young de Soum dogs in the Pyrenees Mountains circa 1930.

breed has been referred to by many names. Le Grand Chien de Montagnes des Pyrénées is the French name, shortened sometimes to Grand Chien des Pyrénées or Montagnes des Pyrénées. In the literature we see dogs referred to as Pyrenean wolf dog or hound and the Pyrenean Bearhound, Pyrenean Mastiff, and others that are reported and assumed by many to be Pyrs.

13

Kurdistan historically covers an area that includes Eastern Turkey, Northern Iraq, North Western Iran, and areas of Syria and Azerbaijan. Ancient Mesopotamia is included in this area. It includes a large mountainous plateau. Literally it is a crossroads to every other part of the world by land and sea. To look at it another way, it would be an ideal candidate for the nomadic migration of early man and his livestock in all directions. The climate in the area is extreme, with cold harsh winters and brutal hot summer days. Tibet is far to the East from Kurdistan.

Kuvasz -- Note the curly coat and absence of double dewclaws.

The path of the sheep migration that Dr. Kovács references from the region goes in all directions, encompassing some of the major mountain chains in every direction.

The spreading of Kuvasz-sized dogs (lighter brighter dog) " is identical with the spreading of domestic sheep both geographically and in time".

In <u>A Kuvasz</u> (The Kuvasz), a Kuvasz breed book published in 1996, notes the following:

"After the domestication of clumsy, defenseless herds of sheep and goats the appearance of livestock guardian dogs was inevitable. Results of archeological digs seem to confirm this theory. Remains of large-size dogs dating back some 2000 years earlier in the same territory accompanied fossils of sheep and goats from the 9th century B.C. excavated

"A Morning Ride" Old Lithograph

in the territory of Northern Iraq. Quite remarkable is the closeness of habitation territory currently occupied by the Kurdish shepherd dogs that are of a perfectly similar appearance as Kuvaszok and the provenance of Dzarmoi dog skull fossils with exceptionally well developed strong jaws and teeth. This type of herd dog bred mostly in white coat colors is regarded by many of the Kynologists as the most original ancient representative of Kuvasz-type dogs. From territories close to the "Fertile Crescent," the early origins place of the domestication sheep and goats together with their canine guards moved to the territories of Asia Minor about 9000 years ago and to East and South Europe and Central Asia some 7000 years ago."

The Basque historian Martin de Ugalde tells us the following about the Basque history:

"Archaeological and ethnographic findings indicate that Basque man evolved from Cro-Magnon man in this area over a period dating from 40,000 year ago until distinct features were

Old lithograph of the Château de Foix at Foix, France

acquired approximately 7,000 years ago. Two thousand years later the sheep, not native to these lands, were introduced and horse and cattle farming came into being, as shown by Adolf Staffe."

In Genesis 4:2 we are told that one of the sons of Adam and Eve, Abel, was a shepherd. It is more than likely that Abel employed flock guardian dogs to help him defend his sheep. In

Luke 2:15 we are told that the shepherds left their flock in the field to see the baby Jesus. Surely they did not leave the sheep without any protection. They likely had flock guardian dogs that could be trusted for short periods of time alone with the sheep. Shepherds are mentioned prominently many times in the bible and in the book of Job it speaks of his sheep dogs. All of our histories are very consistent and in agreement basically.

This would put sheep in the Pyrenees Mountain area at about

Comté de Foix Great Pyrenees bitches circa 1974 in France

3000 B.C., likely accompanied by a "Kuvasz sized" dog (lighter brighter dog). This time frame is completely consistent with Dr. Kovács' information. This places the Pyr or Pyr ancestor likely to be in the Pyrenees about the time of the Sumerian City States and about the time of the invention of writing; in other words at the very beginnings of any civilizations known to world history.

Also, the interesting thing is, we see three different dogs many times occurring in close proximity, sometimes with roles overlapping: the "heavier darker" molossoid Mastiff type guard dog, the "lighter brighter" guard dog, and the little herder shepherd dogs associated in our contemporary times with the "lighter brighter" flock guardian dog. I have used the above terminology in quotes, because I seem to come across it in the literature. The "lighter brighter" dog is the "Kuvasz sized" dog Dr. Kovács references, and the "heaver darker" dog is the Mastiff type dog. Since Dr. Kovács tells us that the Kurdish Sheep guarding dog is a possible ancestor to both the Kuvasz and the Tibetan Mastiff, it could follow that the Tibetan Mastiff might not have been an Pyr ancestor, but possibly a cousin, if you will, both coming down from the "Kurdish Sheep Guarding Dog".

Once the flock guardian dogs arrived in the Pyrenees with the domestic sheep that had migrated in the area, it surely interbred with local dogs and additionally over the next five thousand years, those people who invaded and traded through the region brought many dogs. In this number are the Romans, Phoenicians,

Pyrenean Mastiffs are a much different breed than the Great Pyrenees. A classic Mastiff type breed that has been confused at times with the Great Pyrenees

18

Assyrians, and many more. The lighter brighter dog essentially remained and actually developed over these past five thousand years into the dog in character and phenotype we have today.

The historian J. Bourdette tells us that in 1391 King Charles VI's life was saved by a Pyr, and in 1407 the Counts of Bigorre used Pyrs to guard the Château de

Great Pyrenees at Chateau de Foix in Foix, France

Lourdes. It is assumed that they were so successful, that Pyrs guarded all the other châteaux of the Counts of Bigorre. In 1675 the son of King Louis XIV, the young Dauphin, took a Pyr, Patou, as his friend and brought it back from the Pyrenees Mountains. Two years later the Marquis de Louvois acquired a one year old "Patou" at Betpouey. Subsequently, the Pyr gained favor in the Royal Court and many of the most fashionable estates of the day.

The first Great Pyrenees that led to the establishment of the breed in America was imported by the two sisters Hedges in 1931. The first dog imported by the sisters Hedges was Bazen de Soum, who eventually became an AKC Champion some years later, after

Pyr bitch in the Pyrenees Mountains

he arrived at the kennels of Marjorie Butcher of Cote de Neige fame. Mr. and Mrs. Frances V. Crane were friends of these sisters and fell in love with the dogs. It is fortunate for the breed that Mr. and Mrs. Crane took such an interest. They established Basquaerie Kennels. Mr. and Mrs. Crane imported over 60 dogs from France and saved many dogs from the ravages of World War II. Some people mistakenly say that the Crane's saved the breed from extinction, but that is far from the truth and diminishes many heroic acts by many French men and women during and after the occupation by Germany in World War II. Monsieur Senac-Lagrange and Monsieur Dretzen played a similar role during and after World War I. The breed survived these very hard times, not that far apart in time as history goes, by the love and dedication of these noble Frenchmen. Monsieur Bernard Senac-Legrange is the greatest name in French Pyr history and is the acknowledged greatest expert in the history of the breed. He spent his life on behalf of the breed and other breeds as well.

While the Pyr would have survived World War II without the efforts of Mr. and Mrs. Crane, the contribution made by the Crane's is very important, especially here in North America. Today, spurred on by the emergence of goat and sheep herding, we again see the dog fulfilling its age-old duties again in the fields and pastures. The breed is firmly established now all over the world, as well as many other settings never imagined by those ancient shepherds in the high meadows of the Pyrenees Mountains.

Great American Kennels

This will be a thumbnail mention of just four breeders that I consider the top four Great Pyrenees kennels historically in North America.

Basquaerie

Mrs. Crane with puppy bound for England circa 1947

Mr. and Mrs. Frances V. Crane began with the breed in the early 1930's. Their influence and resolve established the breed in North America. Mrs. Mary W. A. Crane was instrumental in the welfare and fortunes of the breed for the rest of her life. One of Maryann and I's great honors was to know Mrs. Crane and count her as a friend. Mr. and Mrs. Crane did everything for the breed and was a top show kennel as well. They supplied almost everyone else with breeding stock and counseled many over much of the rest of the twentieth century.

They saved much breeding stock from Europe by importing over sixty dogs out of France primarily. Many were imported just to bring them out of potential harms way as Germany was marching through Europe in World War II.

Cote de Neige

Marjorie Butcher with a group of Cote de Neige Great Pyrenees circa 1940s

Mrs. Marjorie Butcher only bred for about ten years, but it was a very important time. She is considered by many to be the most talented breeder that every bred Pyrs in North America. After Pyrs she continued breeding Pembroke Welch Corgi's with equal success and talent. Perhaps Mrs. Butcher's greatest contribution was mentoring Edith Smith at Quibbletown. They remained lifelong friends and Mrs. Smith always sought the counsel of Mrs. Butcher. One of my greatest regrets was not knowing Mrs. Butcher.

Quibbletown

Edith Smith was maybe a genius breeder. She and her husband C. Seaver Smith, affectionately known to us all as Seaver, bred for

over fifty years. The heart and soul of the kennel was Edith and Seaver was the greatest proponent of that fact. Seaver was my mentor the last ten years of his life. While I knew Edith Smith, I never got

Edith Smith with a group of puppies at Quibbletown circa early 1950s

to know her during her life. The genius stopped when she died, but the legacy and gene pool she and Seaver set down for us all endures in so many ways. It is still the most important genetic material for quality typey show dogs, maybe in the world. Without exception, every great show Pyr since the 1980's have one or more of the great Quibbletown stud dogs and/or brood bitches as the most influential ancestor behind the dog or bitch in question or the breeding line in question.

Tip'N Chip

Judith Peavey Bankus Cooper was just a young girl when her parents began breeding Pyrs in 1948. Judy soon took over the breeding and has established what may be the greatest breeding

24

Champion Tip'N Chip Mustang Sally - 2008

program in the history of the breed. It is too early to tell at the moment as she is still very actively breeding. She has two beautiful and talented daughters who follow her footsteps and grandchildren who are potentially coming forward as well. The Tip'N Chip dynasty seems in pretty good shape and history will one day record the total results from a retrospective vantage point.

You can see her beautiful bitch Sally on the back cover of this book and read about Sally's extraordinary capacity as a special Pyr elsewhere in the book. Judy has bred many great ones, probably more than any other breeder. The gene pool is steeped in the finest the breed had to offer, which included the best of Basquaerie, Cote de Neige, and Quibbletown. Judy was always smart enough to use the best and use it to its best advantage. Judy has done it all and also known them all.

There are many contemporary breeders producing outstanding Great Pyrenees. Wonderful people who will continue to be

Judy Cooper shown with Judge C. Seaver Smith at the 1997 GPCA National Specialty.

interested in you and your Pyr the rest of the Pyrs life and maybe your life as well. Most good breeders recognize the value passed to us by these great breeders above. Chances are the good contemporary breeders lines will be steeped in this top historical gene stock.

For a referral to a top breeder, go the Resources section of this book and contact the Great Pyrenees Club of America.

26

A Shepherd's Dog

One minor misconception that is popular today is that the Pyr is a Basque dog. As an ethnic group, the Basque do not claim any ownership to the Pyr at all. The Basque studies program at University of Nevada- Reno confirms this, as well as several Basque web sites both here in North American and Europe. While Basque shepherds have always used the dogs and valued them, it is because they are Shepherds that they value the dogs. It is true that

Shepherds in the Pyrenees Mountains circa 19th Century

Basque shepherds use and value the dogs above all else, but the Basque nation makes no claim to the dog. Aside from the shepherds, they really have no interest or knowledge of the dog as a group. Many shepherds use the dogs and there were other ethnic groups of Shepherds in the region continuously over the five thousand years the Pyr has been in the Pyrenees Mountains. The Basque, due to their culture and inheritance laws seemed to propagate the use of the dogs. Younger sons, who would never inherit any of the family estate, moved along to other parts of the world to make their fortunes. In doing so they took along their very valuable flock guardian dogs wherever possible.

The Pyr always worked with the shepherd, the herding dogs, and other Pyrs as necessary. The great success of the dog is predicated on this model. While the Pyr can work alone for varying periods of time quite successfully, much abuse is perpetuated upon the breed by the misconception that they can be

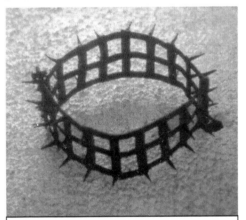

left unattended to work with the livestock. It is a romantic notion by many people who claim some knowledge in the breed, i.e. that the breed is an independent worker. Not

The shepherds fitted the dogs with an iron collar.

true, and they hurt the breed by this stubborn notion as it lends itself to much abuse in the hands of the ill informed who listened to these misguided people and, of course, also the unscrupulous. Now the unscrupulous have backing and validity that leads to abuse of the breed. For the dogs sake this needs to stop. There is a vast difference between dogs working for short periods of time alone in familiar territory with the presence of the shepherds (mankind if you will) and dogs placed out miles from any human contact for many months at a time. Some people would rather stubbornly hold on to their misinformation than to put the welfare of the dogs above their egos. It they would take an honest look at history they cannot find any historical model to support their misguided notion. To compound the problem, some otherwise ethical working breeders buy into this notion. The result is it's not uncommon in the western USA for groups of dogs to be taken far out away from any contact with civilization with herds of animals. The Pyrs only see people a few times a year when they are visited to check on them. Sometime they need to be tranquilized to be given shots and vet care, they are so foreign to human contact. This is abuse!

These people need to invest in a shepherd or find some other way to manage their livestock. Our dogs require more human contact than twice yearly. Many people fail to realize this and it is a romantic notion (no romance for the dogs though) that the Pyr works independently of human interaction. The romance is quickly lost in the face of the abuse that is perpetuated by this misconception.

When the dogs were not in the mountains with the flock they guarded the homes and even villages of the shepherds. You still see village dogs in the Haute Pyrenees area of France today.

The Nature of the Great Pyrenees

This is the second book I have written on the breed plus many articles on the history and nature of the breed. What has struck me when researching the history of the breed is how many people over the ages made great contributions on behalf of the breed. They

were attracted to the breed to an extent that, many times, they devoted their life to little else other than

Phil Oraby with Bonbelle and Jou Jou

the welfare of the breed. Some of these have included the rich and famous.

Mr. and Mrs. Frances V. Crane were wealthy, socially connected and from prominent American families. Monsieur Theodore Dretzen was a Paris newspaper publisher. Le Dauphine, the title given to the young son of King Louis XIV, the "Sun King", brought the Pyr to the Royal French Court at a time of high fashion in French history. There have been many before and since these famous and prominent people, who have taken a very special interest in the Pyr.

There were of course many not so rich and famous. The breed is a peasant's dog that works guarding the flocks. When not in the mountains with the flocks, the Pyr guards the humble shepherd's home and property.

I believe that all God's creatures are very special to him. I also believe that God provided an order and symmetry to his creation. In this order and symmetry, there are special creatures that God set up to aid mankind in his work here on earth.

Nowhere is this special favor exhibited more clearly than with the Pyr, when one studies its history closely. The Pyr and the other Livestock Guardian Dogs have a special place in God's creation. Because of this, God has called many of us to safeguard and look over these special creatures. One of the clearest examples of this stewardship by mankind toward the Pyr is during WWI and WWII in France. So many gave up so much for the welfare and

safeguarding of these special dogs during these very hard times. Monsieur Senac-

Monsieur Andre Delattre with his Pontoise Pyrs at this kennel in Pontoise, France circa 1930's

31

Lagrange and Monsieur Andre Delattre, of Pontoise fame, made great sacrifices during the German occupation on behalf of the breed. Many times they did this to the detriment and safety of themselves.

All the way back through time, the Pyr and its ancestors have given themselves completely for the safety and welfare of

Pyrs go well with small children

mankind. In return, some of us have been called to do the same to ensure that this special creation of God survives and even flourishes for our future welfare. Much the same as the Jews are God's chosen people; Pyrs are one of God's chosen creatures here on earth.

Special Connection

You do not have to be around a Pyr long to know they are something special. Many of us have had dogs and other animals in our lives. They are all very special and have their special place in the creation. I think Pyrs are a bit more special. Pyrs have a

unique connection with all of God's other creatures including man. They are endowed with an intuitiveness and insight into other animals, I am not aware exists in other animals. In addition, they are drawn to the weak, infirmed,

Ruth Graham followed the family Pyr, Belshazzer, running to greet Billy Graham

Photo courtesy Ruth Graham

young, old, injured, or otherwise weakened animals around them. Somehow they can look into the hearts and souls of those around them and see things that it is not possible for other animals to see. They can sense your sadness and your happiness, but they can also tell if a stranger is somehow a threat to you or your property. You find that hard to believe? That is certainly understandable, but talk

33

with any owner, you will hear the same type stories over and over again. They have an unlimited capacity to love and nurture the other animals around them, including mankind, and they have an innate ability to look into the intent of those around them as well.

A beautiful story taking place now as I write this concerns this same breed quality. Sally is a young Pyr, who had her first litter of puppies, just about a week ago, as I write this in the early part of March 2008. Being a maiden with seven puppies under two weeks of age, one would think she had her hands full. Unfortunately, the sire of Sally's puppies was diagnosed with

Emmy with her little buddy Toby.
Owned by Debra Lawrence.

Osteosarcoma a week ago and had his rear leg amputated. The sire of the litter is so very special to the owners, that the ordeal has thrown the family into a difficult time. Normally other animals and certainly the males never get anywhere near new pups. The sire, as are all animals that have gone through such radical surgery, is having a difficult time post op; not only with the physical tasks, but grasping what has taken place in his world so abruptly. Not the least of it is the post op pain, learning how to get on in a weakened state, and learning how to walk on three legs. Many have done it, so even though hard, nothing extraordinary.

Sally took stock of her household and seemed to invite the sire to come lay beside the whelping box, where she and the puppies rested. Sally also will jump up to go out with him, when he needs to go out. He is still having problems walking; she accompanies him and seems to encourage him to move about a bit. After he has

taken care of his business she lays right beside him while he sleeps outside. Usually dams do not leave their puppies but just for a minute or so at this age. She clearly is aware of them, though. Sally also gives support to the family through this very unhappy time in their lives. She leaves the puppies and visits with each of them, as they are available. They are

Correct Pyr head

sure she is ministering to them all.

There are so many stories of the Pyr nurturing the other animals. They can use their amazing sensory perceptions to know when strangers met in passing, are a danger. History records that this trait was recognized so widely at one time, that they were employed in France to ride with the coaches as they traveled over the countryside, which was populated with robbers and murders.

The Pyr was noted for their ability to discern the harmless traveler they would pass, from those who would cause harm.

Your Pyr that lives with you, and/or with your animals, takes all this in its normal activities. It

Penny Lane and Sugar Bear. Owned by Lisa Taylor

encompasses everything within its sight, smell, and earshot as its wards. These sensory areas in your Pyr are extremely keen, and go way beyond our sensory abilities. The point is they know a lot more about what is going on around them than we do. Combine that with their ability to discern the intent of surrounding animals and their needs, you have a very special animal.

Talk with your Pyr

It is a mistake to judge other species in the same manner we judge our species. God did not make it that way and science has a lot to learn about the "why and what for" of all this. I just watched an excellent National Geographic program about one man's ground breaking work with black bears. To me, he is so close to having it right about his communication with this species, it is encouraging. Still, he has been forced to try to judge the bear with the same

Maryann Gentzel with judge Edith K. Smith and Ch. Aneto Benchmark May 6. 1979

criteria we use for humans. That criteria being, self-awareness by the species as some hallmark of intelligence. Pretty amusing, when bears have a sensory system maybe hundreds of times more efficient than ours.

The same applies for dogs in general, but especially for Pyrs. Their sensory system is many times more sensitive and capable than ours in all components i.e. smell, hearing, sight, and an extrasensory component. I do not think we have really identified or certainly have not quantified, any extrasensory components of dog's sensory systems. How else can

37

they know when people are about to have a seizure, a panic attack, or that a stranger poses some danger?

As far as communications, they communicate much better than we do. Our problem is, we do not listen. Even when we listen, I am not sure we really "hear" much of what is said. It's a lot in body language, but there are subliminal areas between them and if we listen carefully, between them and us. I can generally tell you when a dog is happy or sad. I can tell you when it is satisfied or unsettled. My Pyrs give me constant signals of their status and in turn read me like a road map. They know more about our moods and feelings than we many times know ourselves. Same thing exists with the animals in the Pyr's care.

So what exactly am I talking about here? Its not language as we know it. They do not speak English, French, or Greek. We must

have a language to communicate; they do not need one, as we know it. They likely do understand some words in these languages if that is what

Father and son circa 1940's

they have heard. Their language is more body position, facial changes, position of head and tail, some sounds, and other related kinetic communications. There is extrasensory

Estat & Estagel d'Argeles

Two exquisite brothers
imported by Mr. And Mrs. Crane

communication though that humans mostly do not understand. Some of us can get cues and have information imparted to us.

How do I know when my Pyrs are happy with their surroundings? They tell me, clearly. When they are unhappy they let me know. If I do not listen, they will do something about it. They tell us and somehow if we are communicating with the Pyr, we simply "know" and are aware that it came from them. We can begin to read information from them naturally if we want to communicate. They read us almost completely from an early age.

Somehow the Pyr knows when there is any altered state of cognition in us humans. I also think once they observe someone under the effects of drugs or maybe even alcohol, they never forget that person and will never trust them. I have observed this on several occasions.

One of the points of all this is, when our Pyrs tells us they do not like someone, there is a reason. It may be a good reason and important that we should listen very carefully.

Talk with your Pyr. They understand every word and nuance of your character in a cognitive manner that is more important than the actual meaning of the words themselves. Just because God gave them a different set of sensory capabilities that are way beyond our capabilities, we cannot assume they are inferior in any respect. They are just different and what a wonderful difference it is with this breed!

In my first book done in 2002 I printed a tribute to a 15 week old puppy, Abe, who had died a horrible death after suffering for weeks with the after effects of a break through Parvo attack. In looking back at what I wrote in 2000, I can see the talking taking place between my puppy Abe and myself. I will reproduce part of it again here so you can get a feel for the communication that exists between our Pyrs and us.

Abe always kissed everyone. Today as I left him with the vet, just hours from death, Abe said goodbye, to me, with a "flap-flap" of his tail. Always flapping his tail even when moaning in joint pain.

When he felt well enough Abe would talk back to you.
Kind of a high chortle, It said, "I love you."
Dignity and grace in such a little body. Special dog from
a very special breed. His breed beauty was special. His
fighting, loving heart more special.
It hurts so bad to say goodbye to this little Cavalier.
I feel so bad he had to suffer so long in his little life. I
will always remember Abe. Such a special privilege to
know him, even this briefly.
How can such a baby be so courageous?

There was a bit more, but this shows the talk that Abe gave to me even within an hour or so of his death and after suffering weeks with a failure of his immune system secondary to Parvo.

Let me give another example that is a bit different as it is between two classic foes, the Pyr and bear. Several years ago in northern Norway, some bears from a nearby reserve park began coming near town and causing problems for local farmers livestock. During the course of multiple failures to rid the area of the park bears, Pyrs were suggested and were judged to be the wrong animal to rid the area of the visiting bears. This was done by scientists who tested the Pyrs for their aptitude to do this job. Other breeds of dog were used and other measures were tried to keep the bear out of the village without success. Finally, someone decided, let's give the Pyrs a chance, even though they were

41

judged most unsuitable, because they were family dogs and pets from nearby cities. It was observed that the Pyr did at least have a historical reputation to be effective against bear.

You know the rest of the story without me telling it. From the minute the Pyrs went on duty, the bears really ceased to be a problem. The scientists somehow realized that their tests were not applicable to Pyrs, as the tests had been designed for German Shepherds. Our Pyrs flunked their tests, but passed the ultimate test. The Pyrs did get the bears to leave the farms where they returned to the park. The Pyrs certainly talked with the bear and persuaded them to leave the farmer's fields. There were no reported fights, just encounters that resulted in the bear moving away.

Pyrs interacting with bear in Norway.

It was interesting to read another scientist's take on this matter. This scientist dealing with it from an evolution standpoint said the following:

"I'm interested in the evolution of behavior, and in this particular case, the co-evolution (to simply the concept a bit for this brief post) of human and dog behavior. The key fact in this story is that these untrained dogs acted almost entirely as though they were trained protector dogs in how they protected the cattle, harassed the dogs, coordinated their efforts with each other and with the humans, etc.

This is not to say, of course, that I would expect any sort of working dog raised, untrained in their normal 'work' as pets, to do this. I would expect the opposite for most breeds. But this aparently (sic) (from this story and other evidence) is not the case with the Great Pyrenees. This breed appears to come more or less ready out of the box, as it were, to carry out the work the adults normally do in their native setting of alpine cattle lands of the Spanish and French Pyrenees"

I kind of like the description "out of the box." They certainly do come to us ready to do their job, right out of the box. They have been doing this now for over five thousand years. But more importantly to this

Gavernie, one of the many beautiful mountain villages in the Pyrenees Mountains

section, they clearly are communicating with the bear and using only enough force to have the bear leave the farms they have been threatening.

Talk to and listen to your Pyrs. They are continually talking to you. Dr. Doolittle would be proud of you.

"If we could talk to the animals, learn their languages
Think of all the things we could discuss
If we could walk with the animals, talk with the animals,
Grunt and squeak and squawk with the animals,
And they could squeak and squawk and speak and talk to us"

Lyrics from "If I could talk to the animals"

The Decision

Your decision to become a Great Pyrenees owner should not be taken lightly. While Pyrs are an extraordinary animal in many respects, they are far from suitable for everyone. In addition, the decision to have a puppy or an older dog is important to the success of the process. Most reputable Pyr breeders will go to some lengths to make sure you have the right circumstances to successfully be a Pyr owner, but it's necessary that you consider basic elements of the decision.

The breed is from another time and is a living fossil, basically. The Pyr is a primitive dog whose ancestors served primitive mankind at the beginning of his development in basic areas such as keeping domestic animals. From the time of 3000 BC to the present day here in the dawning of the twenty first century, the changes in lifestyle, and the earth are dramatic. A direct descendant of the caveman's dogs living now in the computer

Famous brothers

Champions both

Estat and Estagel d'Argeles

space age, urban sprawl environment is the scenario. I just heard today that for the first time in history, fifty percent of people on the earth live in cities. Exploding populations around the world caused this. If the dog is working livestock or other, maybe more exotic animals, its age-old instincts serve it very well. Other than the traps, poisoning put out by man, and the many pressures of urban life encroaching on the setting, the dog's function much as they have for the past five thousand plus years.

As the dogs come into our home and family they have to adapt

to the urban and contemporary world. What is remarkable about the Pyr

Old French post card

is that it is so adaptable. I think much of this success is because it was always in a constantly changing environment, as the flocks moved often, if not almost continuously. Part of the year the Pyr lived with its shepherd's family guarding the home and family. It was very common for there to be village dogs. The first day Maryann and I were ever in Paris, we saw a Pyr on the Rue du Bac, who lived at a brasserie along the small street. Here was a sort of village dog in the middle of this great city.

Still, there are critical things that need to be considered before bringing a dog into your life, or put to work. Your decision now, before you settle first on a Pyr, and then what Pyr to get, is critical. Failure here will hurt the dog more than it hurts you. Pyrs do not make casual attachments and their allegiances are complete and without bounds. They can change and extend these attachments as they always have, but to take a dog from your home or field to another completely different setting will cause the dog to be confused and unhappy. The Pyr will work no matter where you put it, but to be constantly changing the basic human attachments is a burden faced by so many of our contemporary dogs.

Problem Areas With Pyr Ownership

The potential bad things about a Pyr are:

- Its size

- Its coat

- Its bark

- Its temperament and basic guardian instincts

- Its overbearing instinctual drive

- Its bite

The size aspect is most apparent. It not only will it take up a lot of room; it will position itself to always be in the way. That is a basic part of the guarding behavior i.e. the best vantage point.

The coat sheds a lot. Twice yearly the description of "a lot" is an understatement, as the shedding is immense. Not only that, the coat needs regular upkeep. I believe many of our contemporary dogs have incorrect working coats and require much more upkeep than the original dog that worked in the Pyrenees Mountains.

If the dog is working, this incorrect coat can be a real problem as it can mat to the point that it disables the dog. Shaving the coat is not advised, as the coat that reappears is often impossible to manage. The breed likely will need frequent grooming, not what most working situations are prepared to administer. The correct coat is moderately long and can be a bit undulating, but lies close to the body as the outer or guard coat. The under coat is soft, woolly and keeps the dogs warm and dry during very cold weather or inclement weather, to the point that the dogs actually love the cold and snow. They do not like or want to be wet generally, but the correct coat helps them here as well. When this under coat comes out, the guard coat can trap it. The result can be terrible mats and tangles. This is where the dogs need your attention i.e. to get the shedding undercoat out without it tangling and matting. In

the home, yard, kennel, or field it can look like it snowed at times when the coat is coming out in abundance. A good

Two Pyrs in the Pyrenees Mountains circa 1930's.

thing about the coat is that it is dry (non oily) and self-shedding. Part of the coat care should extend to the nails, especially the double dewclaws. They need trimming. The double dewclaws can grow around and back into the pad that they grew from. This can be severe and disable the dog if let go long enough. One must realize the Pyr is far from being a maintenance free dog.

The bark is huge and frequent. With homes close together, your dog's bark from inside the home can be an annoyance. Don't debark the dog. Just don't get a Pyr. This is not trainable behavior. The only training possible is your being trained to try to minimize the setting that causes the behavior.

The dog's temperament and guardian instincts are at the core of the dog. One of the things that make the Pyr attractive to people drawn to the large, livestock guardian type dogs is the gentle nature of the Pyrs temperament. Some people will tell you that the Pyr has changed over the last fifty years from a less friendly dog to what we have today. That is pure speculation, but it does not matter, unless you have a dog that is not so friendly. Then it's dangerous in our urban world. Ninety five percent of the time the not friendly, fearful, or aggressive behavior is genetic. You will not be able to change it and you certainly do not want to breed it.

The overbearing instinctual drive of the breed to continuously guard can be a big problem in the urban setting. When Pyrs do not have a clear flock, they find one. Mostly it's the family and home and under most circumstances that is fine. There are those situations where the Pyr perceives instinctually that its flock is something else in the area. At that point there is no way to dissuade the Pyr from trying to guard that perceived flock. You may be successful keeping the Pyr from whatever it may be, but the dog will never relent in its attempt to guard that perceived flock. The best one can hope for is to give the Pyr an alternate flock that is more obvious and acceptable. Some of the problems with fencing are the Pyr deciding it must extend its area outside the fenced parameters it guards. We, of course, have no real idea how keen its senses are, but I suspect a Pyr knows for maybe miles what is going on as far as noise and smell is concerned.

Lac de Gaube- High in the Pyrenees Mountains south of Cauterets on the Spanish border. Look closely to see large white dogs in the old photo.

It also has sensory systems that we have no understanding of at all. I am amused when people tell me Pyrs bark at nothing, or at leaves, or butterflies. That never happens. They are barking at something we simply do not know is out there and they are sending their warning out on the airways, if you will, that they are on duty.

Its bite is obvious, but the reasons are not. We expect our dogs to make incredible, rapid decisions, many times in very strange situations. I think it's a wonder they do as well as they do in most of these situations, but when they do bite, it can be a problem. They are so tough, strong, quick, and completely focused on what they do, the results can be very serious. They will not pursue their prey past the point of it being neutralized, but the aftermath of that is not good as well. There are, of course, those dogs that do not make good decisions, or worse dogs that have improper temperaments. There are also dogs that are sick and maybe have neurological problems. I have been told that epileptic dogs can bite. Mental illness or confusion is not unheard of in the dogs as well. All this can result in biting. As I have said already, it's a wonder our dogs do as good as they do, being such ancient, primitive creatures existing in our urban society and being owned by some of the nut cases who are attracted to our noble Pyrs.

One must realize the above things are not the only ones, but some of the main ones that people must factor into their decisions. Good breeders will also force you into awareness of these areas as well, and be there to help you and the dog when it is needed.

Breed attributes

Now that I have properly scared you from ever wanting a Pyr, we can talk about the many attributes of the breed. There are too many to list really, but I will list some of the more important ones to many people.

- It is large
- It is white
- It has a huge bark
- It has a long double coat
- It is calm
- It is friendly with other animals, especially small animals
- It is a companion and quite nurturing in its behavior
- It has a special affinity for the frail, sick, handicapped, small, young, or any way infirmed creatures of any description.
- It is beautiful
- It has a special sense that allows it to interact with mankind in a special way
- It is comical
- It provides safety
- It does not take a lot of maintenance
- It is a low energy dog
- It does not require large amounts of food

- It thrives in outdoors especially cold and winter environs
- It has a dignity and regal ness that is admired by all that know it

Champion Aneto Etienne

It is a large dog. In a working environment, size is necessary to be a one on one combatant with its classic enemy, the European Grey Wolf. It can stand its own in battle with many predators including man. A group of them can combat the largest bears, the large cats and other predators. Many of us like the large dogs and they are a real attraction.

It is white. The white color is important to many situations. In low light it can be seen easier. The white color reflects the heat from the sun and the glare off snow. It is beautiful.

It has a huge bark. The bark is one of its main tools in keeping predators away and warning intruders. It gives notice to all within hearing that they are present and if they proceed they may have to deal with the Pyr.

It has a long double coat. The coat gives it warmth and protection from the elements. The full coat provides additional protection to the body during any encounter. The healthy coat that is maintained is beautiful.

The Great Pyrenees as an adult is a calm breed, as breeds go. For that reason it works well indoors, with children, and older adults. For a large dog, it can do very well in apartments and areas where there is not a lot of exercise room. It does not require large amounts of exercise to burn off its natural energy, as do many breeds.

Dixie, Penny Lane, and Sugar Bear, not quite working? Owned by Lisa Taylor.

The Great Pyrenees gets along very well with other animals especially small animals whether they be canine or other. For example, they are a good dog to have around cats. It is very common for the small dog in the household to "rule" the Pyr and this may be one exception to not putting two adult males together. If there is a problem here, it will likely be the fault of the small macho male dog, but even then, most Pyrs will in frustration give just one big "woof" and maybe a shove or nip to stop the aggravation.

Great Pyrenees are legendary for their association with old and infirmed people. They are also noted to be very nurturing to young animals, even newborn animals that are abandoned in the field. I have noticed that creeping and crawling infants make them nervous when they move directly toward them and sometime they growl, but mostly move away from the infant. Past that, the family Pyr is generally fine with all ages of the children.

A Friendly Gesture

Attributed to Herring, Sr- 1847

The Great Pyrenees also has special affinity for the frail, sick, handicapped, small, young, or any way infirmed creatures of any description. This goes right along with the prior paragraph. If they did not shed so much, they would be a great dog for the blind and handicapped.

Only God could give us such an exquisite creature that is a superb rugged protector. It's God's blessing on the breed and on us. The Pyr's great beauty is known by all. The beauty is in part the outward manifestation of its value and usefulness to man now really from the cradle of mankind. We are all proud of our lovely Pyrs and its beauty attracts many to the breed.

They can be quite comical, but others, than owners of the breed, rarely see this amusing side of the Pyr. Because of their guardian behavior they are rather stoic and reserved around others. In the family they can be quite funny and have a personality that can be mischievous in an innocent way. It is a special privilege when a Pyr displays this behavior around you and this behavior is reserved for those it loves and protects.

The safety it provides is obvious. It does this in all settings that

**Ch. Quibbletown Cinderella with the Selbert Twins circa 1950's.
Cinderella was the first Champion Pyr with a UD obedience degree.**

it lives. If allowed it will also provide safety for your neighbors.
Many times your neighbors are not so happy about this as they do
not understand, or maybe they do not want strangers barked at as
they approach their homes. So this is not recommended and one of
the major reasons fencing is required. People enjoying the
outdoors will enjoy their Pyr for many reasons. One of the big
reasons is the safety they bring along. I think that a lot of these
poor people and children who are kidnapped and harmed would
have been safe had a Great Pyrenees been part of the equation.
Certainly, the dog would have had to be killed in order to get to the

child or adult. That in its self might provide the mechanism for escape. The dog historically is noted for its innate ability to determine friend from foe in strangers. The Pyr was used at one time in France to accompany the coaches traveling overland. In a time when many travelers passed along the byways were robbers and murders, the Pyr was considered quite valuable to be on board the overland coach.

On a humorous note, I have been told of families who had Pyrs for some time, would have to have their young daughter's new suitors meet the Pyr first. If they passed the Pyr test they could take the daughter out. This is funny, but God has given the Pyr the ability to discern, many times, evil intent in people. At the least, a Pyr should be given some credence when it suddenly does not like a stranger. Those dogs who normally do not bark when they get the vibes from its owner that all is OK, but then suddenly acts different toward particular strangers, are the ones to be careful. Your Pyr may know something that you do not.

Other than its coat, the maintenance required is low. It does not require a lot of food to be healthy. Its metabolism is low and this likely accounts for the low energy and low food requirements. Over the five thousand years it has existed and before, with its ancestors, these large dogs needed to be able to guard and fight if necessary, many times on little or no food. Natural selection left us with dogs that could be successful with less nutrition up to a point. That is why many Pyrs naturally will be slim or downright skinny even when abundant food is available. For a breed they are a poor eater. They are healthy as breeds go also. With a shorter working coat and attention to dew claws the Pyr really needs very little except proper nutrition, and this is mostly not a large volume of food for its size. A Spaniel or Retriever will eat much more than a Pyr. I am not advocating not feeding your dogs a good diet. See the section on food and feeding. I am only noting its historical capacities and aptitudes.

Group of Comte de Foix Great Pyrenees at Foix, France circa 1950,s

Pyrs love the outdoors especially in the winter. The weather cannot get too cold for a Pyr and they act downright silly around snow. Here you will definitely see the clown emerge.

Everyone who knows one and certainly those who live with one appreciates the dignity of the Great Pyrenees. As the dog ages and enters the frail stage of life, one has to admire their grace and dignity in the face of their failing body. You see this also in disabled dogs. They simply pick up and go if they can, even if they need help. The old frail dog will be out guarding or trying to do so if allowed. They never stop, never. They teach us a lot by example.

Great Pyrenees as Livestock Guardian Dogs

Great Pyrenees guarding sheep in the Pyrenees Mountains

Great Pyrenees are excellent livestock guardian dogs for obvious reasons. That is their core feature and the single most important reason we have them in the first place. Pyrs have been guarding livestock (flocks) now for over five thousand years and before that their direct ancestors did the same job for another six thousand years, at least. This association goes back to the beginning of man's endeavors with livestock and the need to protect the livestock and man himself, from the ravages of predators. Some things never change much and even though the predators have come and gone and the livestock have become much more varied, our Pyrs have shown a remarkable quality of adapting to each situation.

Since 1972 I have placed over 70 dogs in working situations, mostly in small pastures in the southeastern USA. I guess because I started doing this with farmers so long ago when I was alone essentially in the whole region, I never knew what others might have told me was not possible or advisable. The dogs have taught me all that I know and it is a remarkable record in that I know of no failure of one of my dogs to work. Were there some problems along the way? Yes, of course, but each was fairly easy to solve. Sometimes we did not initially give the dog in question the benefit of the doubt and its seeming failure actually was not one at all. For example, the very friendly young male who went to work at a southern agriculture college in the mountains of Kentucky had begun to experience losses from predators when they called me. This young dog, from a strictly show line had been a show dog, but his one traveling testical, after going up and back down several times, decided to stay up. The college called and he went at about a year old to work for a living. He was very friendly and loved the attention from the students. I began to get calls that he was not staying with the livestock, as he wanted to visit with the students. We worked on this for several weeks without seeming success. He also found a neighbor who really liked him and would let him ride in his truck. All these things are not particularly good things for a livestock guardian dog. After weeks of failure and about to give up and bring him home to live here in the kennel, I asked the question: "Are you loosing any livestock since this has been going on?"

After a pause, the answer was; "Well, no. But I am afraid we might." Good point! Next I asked if he spent time with the livestock? It was determined that he did spend considerable time with the livestock; he just liked to visit and play some. I knew this little guy pretty well and wondered if he had it under control. We just did not know it because he did not fit the mold we wanted. By now he had the nickname, "playboy". What we decided to do was to watch him closely and see if his playing would result in livestock losses. The answer was no, to my knowledge, it never did. The point of this is not to dispute the conventional wisdom, but to look carefully at these dogs. They have such ancient instincts that to date are so ingrained in their being; that these instincts determine most of what Pyrs do naturally. We mostly screw them up with our sometimes misguided notions about what should be or what we want.

Most of the dogs I have placed have been older, as much as seven years old in one case. What is important is that the dogs recognize their "flock." When you observe these dogs very closely you will see that they guard anyway, even if they do not have a job. Instinctively they have to pick something to guard. It's what they are all about and for their whole life they do nothing other than guard, and those attributes associated like nurturing, and being in tune with everything around them. In most cases they do this so benignly that we never realize just how hard they are working. This is a 24/7/365 job. They never take a vacation and never call in sick. Whether they work with other dogs or do it all themselves, it makes no difference. Their strengths are part

Chevy with his sheep and goats. Chevy is a Canadian Champion, so he is a working dog and a show dog. Owned by Brian and Susan Price.

of their problem. They do their job so good, some people begin to imagine that they can do it all by themselves. While they can, sometimes for short periods of time and will never really fail, they suffer without complaints or noticeable problems. They never say "No!"

The traditional knowledge says that a Pyr must be raised with the livestock. The old French axiom says something like; raised with the flock and suckle the milk of the ewe, which would indicate they begin the "bonding" before they are weaned. Some will tell you they cannot have much, if any human contact. Traditionally the dogs went out with the flocks in the spring and came back with them in the fall in the ancient practice of Transhumance still being practiced in France. In the interim they guarded the home of the shepherd. While being out from spring to fall, the flock moved continuously grazing. All this dictated a dog that is very adaptable to many different settings and situations. So it's no surprise they are so adaptable even in our urban settings. Never forget, even though you may think they are doing nothing or just hanging out at your home, they are guarding every second of their lives once they begin this instinctual process as a young dog. Can we screw them up or make them so neurotic that they cannot function normally. You bet we can! Are there seriously flawed dogs bred as far as their temperaments are concerned that cannot work. Yes, certainly there are.

A properly bred dog with proper temperament will guard naturally. This natural behavior can start at any age. The most important thing is for the dog to identify and understand where and who is its flock. After that, some basic common sense things like, do not entice the dog to leave its flock for companionship, food, etc. Dogs can visit, but make sure it is always expected that they return to their flock.

Ninety to ninety five percent of what they do is "mark and bark." Pretty simple it seems, but a lot more than is apparent went into that equation of success. Predators respect the dogs and the dogs tell them way before they even attempt to enter their area that they are on duty. Most predators take this seriously and look for an easier meal somewhere else. Those who do not have to deal with the dogs and that is as sure as the sun rising every morning. The hardest thing you as a shepherd (owner) has to do is determine what is needed by the

Great Pyrenees ministering to its flock

circumstances i.e. the area covered, the type(s) of predators, and the numbers of predators. Dogs can be overwhelmed and this generally results in the death of the dog as he normally stands and fights to protect the flock no matter what the odds are against him. The more cunning predators like the coyote know when the numbers are in their favor and play games with the dogs like, luring them to one end of the pasture with part of their pact while some others attack the flock. They just need a few minutes opening. So maybe another dog or so in the pasture will solve this problem, as the dogs seem somehow to magically divide up the work. Some stay with the flock while the others patrol or engage.

I am going to give some very generalized guidelines that will work most of the time. There will be some exceptions, but most of these can be worked with successfully. There are some very good web sites and other information on the Internet that is generally reliable. There is also a Livestock Guardian Dog chat list on the web that can be a good resource for information and advice on

Two Pyrs working at my friend Benoît Cockenpot's goat dairy farm, in his high pasture in the Pyrenees Mountains.

specific problems. If you will "goggle" it, you will find it easily.

Before I list the guidelines, lets talk just a bit about the dog itself. Remember, I said almost all dogs work fine, at least to my knowledge, is the state of the breed to date here at the beginning of 2008. That might change and left to mankind likely will down the road. Buy a reasonably well-bred dog. See the section on buying your dog. One that the breeder has taken at least some time to consider what they are doing as opposed to just finding the cheapest most available dogs and breeding them. Your biggest problem here, which we will cover more in the health and genetic section, are health and genetic problems. Some of these affect the dog's ability to work successfully. Also, unless you plan to be very serious about breeding and truly study the breed and its genetics, leave that to someone else. There are other very important considerations about breeding that need factoring into this decision as well. See the section on breeding.

Guidelines for selecting a Livestock Guardian Dog

Select a dog from stock that has done at least minimal health clearances on both parents and in the case of using an outside stud dog, insisted that a stud dog also has the minimal health clearances. Minimal health clearances are a grade of fair or better on OFA examined hips and absence of Patella subluxation. These, both of them, should be published somewhere like the OFA web site to allow independent verification of same. These are both serious problems in the breed. They are one of the most common genetic disorders seen in the breed. When these problems occur in working dogs they can be very disabling and stop the dog from doing its job and cause much pain and suffering for the dog if left to struggle with the disability. The dog will likely ignore and struggle through the pain or infirmity, as it will not stop working.

With an older dog the same applies if you are dealing with a breeder. If you are taking a dog from rescue, you need to have the knees and hips looked at by a good Vet. While at the Vet have them look at the whole dog as well. Shoulders and hocks can be a problem also. Have them look at the eyes and heart as well. They likely cannot do what a specialist can do, but you are better off having that look while the dog is there. If you cannot have these done or get his information, don't take that dog. Unfortunately, there are many dogs now and you can find a healthy dog to work and that is what you must have.

Spay or neuter any Pyr you get.

Prefer the dog from a breeder who is healthy and they know a lot about the good health of their breeding line as opposed to the farmer who mostly touts his dog are "working stock", but know little or nothing about

Do you think Pyrs are in tune with their flock?

70

the health. Sometimes they are one and the same, even better. Truth is, all Pyrs work essentially, so the farmers claim does not mean very much really. You should prefer the dog from the breeder even if they, the breeder, professes to know nothing about working dogs and even may be adverse to same. In the long run you will be better off as you can get help with your dog from others even if your breeder is afraid or not eager to do this. This is simply ignorance of one area and the breeder maybe has lost sight of the reason they were able to get the breed in the first place i.e. it was such a successful working dog for so long. Sometimes the show world gets a little carried away with itself, but they are good folks who love the breed a great deal and have fabulous dogs that will be fabulous dogs on your farm and with your family.

Color or sex makes no difference other than personal preferences.

Smaller puppies in a litter can and most of the time grow up to be quite suitable. Even a smaller adult Pyr will work fine. The old saying that "its not the size of the dog in the fight, but the size of the fight in the dog that is important," applies here. There is plenty of fight in the Pyr of any size. By fight I refer to the whole instinctual guardian dog package.

Coat is the one area that I find real fault with us show breeders. We have many times bred a coat that is incorrect in order to be able to groom it out and win under our judges who many times do not understand the working attributes of the breed. Some of these huge coats that become more profuse with spaying or neutering, will be a real problem for the working dog. They tangle and mat so easily they are a problem to keep acceptable. Shaving them is not the answer as the coat mostly comes back much worse or impossible to manage. Try to find a dog with a shorter coat that is flat (as opposed to stand off as one sees in the Samoyed breed). Otherwise you will be spending a lot of time brushing or combing out the incorrect coat or paying someone to do same. The flat outer or guard coat that lays down, even if long, will work fine and need minimal care over the life of the dog.

There will be a few other things of a minor nature to crop up, but these are the main areas you need to consider.

The Pyr when you bring it home to the livestock?

Your number one priority is to have the dog get comfortable with the livestock and vice versa. They need to quickly relate to the animals they will be guarding. The animals must know the dogs are suppose to be there and are safe to have around them. The scenario is not much different for dogs that have seen animals and those who have never seen a farm animal.

Lets start with a puppy maybe as young as 7 weeks old. It is going to be very unhappy, under any circumstances, being separated from its littermates for the first time. It does not need to get in extreme cold or heat, at least for a while. Put the puppy near the livestock in a suitable enclosure where it can see the animals, but cannot get out. Give it what you would give a puppy. A blanket or bedding, something to play with and chew upon, plenty of top quality food and always an abundance of fresh water are

things the puppy needs. Let a puppy stay there for a few weeks and then begin letting it in with some of the gentler livestock,

Historically, the wisdom was to start the pups with the sheep at a very early age.

but do not let it try to play or chew on any of the animals. A gentle "no" reminder repeated often is enough. Keep it this way for months. You might begin to see some guardian behavior at as early as four months. There is a safety issue with the pups, as large livestock or older ewes; etc can be dangerous to these little puppies. So keep it light and short for awhile. You will know when the dog can be left longer, but never tolerate any pestering of the farm animals. Strictly forbidden and correction always required. One day soon all will click in place and it will never happen again. Every time there is a failure, go back one step and start over. A sameness routine and being consistent is what is required. Gentle firmness that is always consistent is the cardinal rule. You may be surprised how easy it is. For those difficult cases, stay vigilant, the pay off is around the corner and the rewards are great. Do not let young adolescent Pyrs get abused by any of the stock. The Pyr memory is very long. Pyrs will remember and retaliate. So if you have a very bossy Ewe with lambs, keep the adolescent from them until they are mature and until the time when the Ewe would never challenge the dog. If you get into a situation that you cannot solve, ask for help. That is where the Livestock Guardian List on the web might be a great resource.

Older dogs are much the same. It's amazing to see the ancient instincts surface naturally and normally. Almost like unwrapping a package. The routine is basically the same minus the puppy behavior considerations. They should progress much faster as well. So many times I hear after they took the older dogs from my place, put it in the pasture and made sure everyone was fine with each other that the job was done. Generally the day the Pyr enters the pasture full time is the day that you will stop loosing livestock to predators. The change is amazing. It never ceases to excite me to hear it over and over again from the people who take these wonderful dogs and allow them to bloom into what their ancestors have done so naturally for the past five thousand years.

Problems? Yes, of course, sometimes. If a dog wants to dig out or gets out, it either has not bonded properly with the livestock or perceives something on the outside it believes requires its attention. Remember drop back one step and begin again. Put it in a secure enough area right in the middle of the livestock as possible or as near to it as one might. It needs at a minimum, to be just adjacent where it can sniff and be sniffed by the livestock. Another reason for digging or otherwise defeating fencing to escape is the dog is seeing, smelling, or hearing something outside the fence that its instincts tell it to either investigate or deal with. You are going to have to work on this. Sometimes a good strong hot wire will solve the problem and is easy, safe, and cheap. Usually the battery powered ones are not enough adverse stimuli to faze a Pyr. As a rule invisible fencing is useless.

The goal is for the Pyr to become attached to the livestock in such a way that it does not want to be anywhere else, or at least it is sure all is well with its livestock during brief absences.

No hot wire or fence will replace that attachment and it is a natural one that will come from deep inside the dog itself. These external things do help though, so use them to get to the place you want your Pyr to be.

Occasionally you will come across a dog that is not suitable. I have not seen this yet, but I trust some who have reported this to know they do exist. I suspect these Pyrs might work with another Pyr who is a good worker. That subject is way beyond the scope of this book.

We have talked about the Pyr working with the shepherd and the little herding dogs. Mostly here in North America they work with Border Collie type dogs. These are great dogs and the Pyr seems to get along with them fine. In France and Europe the Pyr traditionally works with

Rough Faced (Long coat) variety. Note the long coat tends to cord.

the Pyrenean Berger or Shepherd. There is a Rough Face (long coat) and Smooth Face (short coat) variety. They may be two

different breeds, but are interbred. They have been imported here to North America. The Canadian Kennel Club recognizes them and my understanding is the AKC will do so maybe this year (2008) or in 2009.

Smooth Face (Short Coat) variety

One last word about your working Pyr. Their job is guarding your livestock. While they can have a tolerance to humans that are not part of the family group, it is asking too much of them to be friendly with every neighbor, not immediate family member, and friends who may want to drop by and see the "Pyr work". It is normal for them to bark or act aggressively to those who have no reason to be in their field except to satisfy their curiosity. The Pyr has to make a lot of decisions as it is, so lets not saddle them with the requirement that they must have some supreme ability to decide which of these strangers is appropriate in their field. If you get a Pyr that stays in the field with the livestock and prevents predators, the Pyr has done its job. If the Pyr does not like you father in law, the cousins kids, and the neighbors in-laws in their field, that is the way it is. They are still succeeding in their job as protector of your livestock. If you have to have all this traffic through your place maybe you should not have livestock or Pyrs? Workers and people who's regular presence is necessary will be viewed as such by your Pyr and allowed access in a reasonable manner. If you have occasional situations with other workers needing to get in or adjacent to the area, consider putting your Pyr away. Neighbors should understand these are serious working dogs and that their access needs to be by specific understanding and invitation only.

The AKC Standard --the Ideal Working Great Pyrenees.

It is surprising that such a superb working dog that has such a great appreciation in the dog show world seldom have these two areas appreciated together. The danger of this is that the show breeders will change the breed to suit its fashion and the working breeders will not have the historical perspective to breed the correct Pyr. In either hands the wonderful dog that attracted us all to it, could eventually be lost or diminished in some aspects.

Working dogs have difficulty competing in the show world as the show world wants them too fat and with too much coat that is ideally kept flawless. The best one can hope for is breeders who understand and revere both settings and produce litters that can both work and compete with the best of them in the show ring. A good breeder will have a lot of homogeneity in their breeding. Some dogs can do both in a limited manner, or do one part of the time and the other part of the time.

A working dog is the pure essence of the Pyr, a very ancient, natural breed that developed over at least five thousand years and very likely developed functionally from their ancestors used as flock guardian dogs the prior six thousand years. I know this is redundant, but it is important and warranted by its redundancy. The Pyr historically and foremost is a working dog! It is the sole reason we have this erstwhile breed today.

Traditionally the Pyr was employed with the flocks, but it has also found itself equipped to work in many settings. It always guarded the homes and huts of shepherds, hence, one of its nick names of "Mat Dog"-- the name given because you always found your Pyr in front of the door, probably blocking the passage way. Those who own Pyrs are well accustomed to the Pyr in your home, most likely lying in front of a door in the house. If the Pyr can, it will lie so the door must open onto it.

For you working enthusiasts, or those interested in the working attributes of the Pyr, I am taking some selected portions of the AKC standard of the breed and documenting and illustrating how these attributes make this a very special dog equipped very well to do its job. A job with about five thousand years of success. That is now used worldwide for its excellent and very successful abilities. No doubt, it is the ecologically preferred way to control predators for all livestock.

I am selecting some portions that it is easy to assume they are just part of a "beauty contest". The quoted parts of the standard for the breed will be in bold italics.

The AKC standard opens telling us:

The Great Pyrenees dog conveys the distinct impression of elegance and unsurpassed beauty combined with great overall size and majesty.

The most general problem seen in working Pyrs is their incorrect phenotype. Many times they look more like the heavier mastiff type dogs we spoke of earlier. The elegance is the end result of "form following function natural development" that occurred. The elegance and size are important in taking on the predators. You will see a bit later that elegance is the result of the breed characteristics needed to be the best at its job.

Substance - The Great Pyrenees is a dog of medium substance whose coat deceives those who do not feel the bone and muscle. Commensurate with his size and impression of elegance there is sufficient bone and muscle to provide a balance with the frame.

Faults: Size - Dogs and bitches under minimum size or over maximum size. Substance - Dogs too heavily boned or too lightly boned to be in balance with their frame.

We know we need a big dog, but that is so many times confused with heavy and ponderous. The Pyr needs the size, but the ability to be very quick and fast in chasing predators or getting to the predators, before they can attack the livestock. Medium substance will do this much better than the heavier larger bone dogs so many mistakenly want. There are other guardian breeds that fill that bill if one wants a heavy, large boned and headed dog. The Great Pyrenees is not that dog. You want a dog that is large, powerful, fast, and agile. They need to cover ground at a high speed. Check out the Pyr in the series of pictures above. This Pyr is covering some ground. One can see the speed, power, and agility this dog possesses. The dog needs to be big enough to take on big predators successfully, but not fat or heavy.

Eyes - Medium sized, almond shaped, set slightly obliquely, rich dark brown. Eyelids are close fitting with black rims.

The eye size is important, as is the tight eyelid. The dogs work in blowing snow, debris, and even sand. Large open eyes that are loose would be a constant problem for foreign matter to become trapped causing constant irritation

The black rims act as glare control, especially in the snow, much as an athlete playing under bright light uses black under the eyes for same.

Glare off the snow is a problem that the dark rims around the eyes help.

The oblique angle is further enhancement of the tight eye feature.

The amber brown color is efficient for the opaqueness of the light traveling into the eye in a variety of different lighting situations. The Pyr works historically, most actively at night, in dawn, and in dusk light conditions. These are all low light conditions. With eye color, we are talking about the iris of the eye. The iris is an adjustable diaphragm around the aperture of the pupil. It assists with the amount of light entering the eye by changing the size of the pupil. The color is determined by the amount of melanin found in the iris. The darker the eye color, the more melanin found in the iris. One of the functions of melanin in the iris is to help absorb excess light that might otherwise overwhelm our vision. Albinos, who lack melanin, have great problems in bright light environments. The iris actually is part of the choroid, a layer of cells that surround the eyeball. The retinal cells that are responsible for sensing light from the environment are located on the top of the choroid cell layer. This may explain, at least partially, why blue eyes occur in people from more northern climates with less light intensity. Conversely, higher light intensities, in more equatorial regions, seem to result in dark eyed people. These people tend to have dark skin, dark hair, and dark eyes. The Pyr works, historically, at higher elevations with some higher light intensities and increased UV ray intensity. It also has the problem of glare associated with snow. I believe most importantly the need to see well in nighttime, early evening and dawn conditions is assisted by a component of the amber seen in the dark brown. The Pyr seems suited with a condition of moderation of iris pigmentation for light extremes. There are high light conditions but the need for lower light conditions as well. That is why you do not want yellow eyes (too much light) or black eyes (less light). The dark brown with the amber high lights seems to be a middle position best suited for the various conditions the Pyr encountered historically.

Ears - Small to medium in size, V-shaped with rounded tips, set on at eye level, normally carried low, flat, and close to the head. There is a characteristic meeting of the hair of the upper and lower face which forms a line from the outer corner of the eye to the base of the ear.

This picture represents ideally the eyes and ears of a very correct working Pyr. In fact the whole headpiece is exemplarity for correct breed type. This happens to be a French dog, but we have many excellent examples of the breed here in America.

In some of the similar type

white guardian dogs they crop the ears as they sit too high upon the head and are a prime target for the predators to mangle. One of the nice things about a Pyr is the lovely ears sit back on the side of the head, ideally hidden in the abundant fur. The prior dog picture has about the most correct head one can imagine. Note the position of the ears, clearly out of the way, should he get into a skirmish with a predator.

Skull and Muzzle-The muzzle is approximately equal in length to the back skull. The width and length of the skull are approximately equal. The muzzle blends smoothly with the skull. The cheeks are flat. There is sufficient fill under the eyes. A slight furrow exists between the eyes. There is no apparent stop. The boney eyebrow ridges are only slightly developed. Lips are tight fitting with the upper lip just covering the lower lip. There is a strong lower jaw. The nose and lips are black.

This shaped head will have a more powerful jaw than a square head. This is purely the law of levers and angles from physics. The jaw and its muscular attachments make up a class three lever. In this type of lever, the longer the lever arm, the more power that is generated. This class lever will amplify motion. The resultant power is the product of speed and strength (force). In short, the longer muzzle will generate more power than a shorter muzzle.

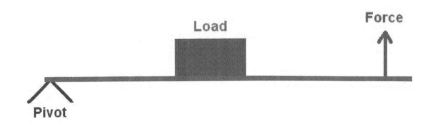

Third Class Lever

The shepherds did not want a square head with a short muzzle for very important reasons.

In addition, the tight lips and what is almost a "V" shaped muzzle allow for infighting much better that a blunter wider muzzle.

Correct head and expression are essential to the breed. The head is not heavy in proportion to the size of the dog. It is wedge shaped with a slightly rounded crown.

The slightly rounded crown to the head, plus the occipital protuberance in concert with the muzzle shape, give added power to the bite, exerted by this headpiece. The prior AKC standard spoke of the occipital protuberance and the French Standard speaks of "the occipital protuberance is apparent, the back of the skull is ogival shape." The term ogival is one denoting the shape seen in stained glass windows in French Churches and is an inverted "V" shape for the occipital protuberance. The larger the occipital protuberance the more wedge or "V" shaped the head and the stronger the power of the bite.

86

Flat headed, wide muzzled, with loose lips, presents a dog with less efficient headpiece to do its job.

Suddenly one can appreciate in the beauty this correct head presents in the phenotype is functionally a very powerful efficient system of dealing with large strong predators.

Teeth - A scissor bite is preferred, but a level bite is acceptable. It is not unusual to see dropped (receding) lower central incisor teeth.

Good teeth need little explanation and in this case a picture is worth a thousand words.

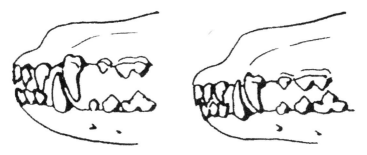

Tail - The tailbones are of sufficient length to reach the hock. The tail is well plumed, carried low in repose and may be carried over the back, "making the wheel," when aroused. When present a "shepherd's crook" at the end of the tail accentuates the plume.

You might ask, what in the world could its tail have to do with its working? When you see a flock of sheep, the Pyr many times will be right in the middle of them. Difficult or impossible to tell the dog from the sheep at any distance and in poor light i.e. in twilight and darkness it's impossible. When the dog is alert the tail

 is wheeled over its back. When the dog is relaxed, if it has the shepherds crook, the "flip" of the tail is fairly easy to see to know there is a dog in the flock. If there is danger or the dogs are actively guarding, the tail will be wheeled over its back and when the shepherd is joining into the skirmish, he will stand a better chance of not striking or hitting the dog, if he can clearly identify the Pyr. So it is important to the shepherd for identification and some added safety for the Pyrs.

The weather resistant double coat consists of a long, flat, thick, outer coat of coarse hair, straight or slightly undulating, and lying over a dense, fine, woolly undercoat. The coat is more profuse about the neck and shoulders where it forms a ruff or

mane which is more pronounced in males. Longer hair on the tail forms a plume. There is feathering along the back of the front legs and along the back of the thighs, giving a "pantaloon" effect. The hair on the face and ears is shorter and of finer texture. Correctness of coat is more important than abundance of coat.

Faults: Curly coat. Stand-off coat (Samoyed type).

The Pyr coat is one area that needs work. We are seeing too many of the stand-off coats mentioned as a fault, and it is getting past too many judges without being penalized. The result is a coat that traps the undercoat as it sheds causing tangles and huge mats. These at some point will cause the dog to break down in its working and just as bad, cause the coast to be clipped down, which should never occur. The coat actually helps the dog in heat situations. Also when it's clipped many times it comes back in so incorrect with a soft wooly undercoat texture that mats easily traps dirt and debris, almost like sponge traps water. The correct outer guard coat is coarse, dry, lays flat, and sheds dirt and loose hair that falls out from the undercoat. That is what we want and has always been one of the strengths of the Pyr coat that made it very desirable as a flock guardian dog. Jay Russell, PhD has documented why the white long coat is actually better for the dog in the heat than one shaved down. He has demonstrated this information via physics and presents a mathematical formula for calculating the values using Newton's Law of cooling.

White or white with markings of gray, badger, reddish brown, or varying shades of tan. Markings of varying size may appear on the ears, head (including a full face mask), tail, and as a few body spots. The undercoat may be white or shaded.

We want a principally white dog, but color on part of the body is fine. We have already seen why white is important for weather conditions. A Pyr in the middle of the flock can become almost lost. You have to look just a bit to find the Pyr in the picture below. I am not sure the animals care much about color, but there are reasons we care. The weather makes white a very good color especially is it self sheds, as does the Pyr's coat.

Its easy to miss the Pyr lying with the sheep

Character and temperament are of utmost importance. In nature, the Great Pyrenees is confident, gentle, and affectionate. While territorial and protective of his flock or family when necessary, his general demeanor is one of quiet composure, both patient and tolerant. He is strong willed, independent and somewhat reserved, yet attentive, fearless and loyal to his charges both human and animal

The Pyr has historically been a dual purpose dog i.e. they work the flocks in the spring, summer, early fall, and guard the homes of the shepherds the rest of the fall and winter. They have developed a very compliant temperament and should be adaptable and friendly enough to be in a village, without danger to those who live and visit the village. Shy dogs work the flock fine, it's the rest they do not do well and that is not correct Pyr behavior.

Grey Wolf (Canis Lupus)

The European Wolf is a subspecies of the Grey Wolf (Canis Lupus) seen in North America. They once were seen America. Today the Grey Wolf can only be found in Canada, north Michigan and Wisconsin in the USA, also in

Russia, and pockets of east Europe. They can be 7 feet long (including the tail which is less than half the body length) and weigh up to 175 pounds. They are a carnivore. I don't think it is any coincidence that the full grown, mature adult male Pyr approaches and approximates the size of the Wolf. Anything else would have failed and probably did. They are the classic foe of the Pyr.

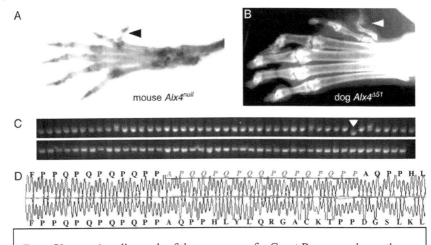

Dew Claws: A radiograph of the rear paw of a Great Pyrenees shows the typical double dewclaw phenotype specified in the breed standard (arrowhead). (C) Polydactylous Great Pyrenees are homozygous for a 51-nucleotide repeat contraction in the Alx-4 gene. PCR amplification of the repeat-containing regions of Alx-4 from 89 dog breeds reveals that this deletion is unique to the Great Pyrenees breed (arrow).

Dewclaws have little use if any. Historically it was considered a sign of purity of breeding and that is its value. There were and still are so many crosses that the purity of the breed was threatened at various times in its very long history. Truth is, there are a lot of other dog's blood mixed in our dog's background, but the purity of the breed has survived and thrives today. There is new evidence that was published by the National Academy of Sciences in December 2004. It has to do with repeat of alleles on the Alx-4 gene. See above. We are grateful to the National Academy of Sciences for this information.

As we end this section, we note that a Pyr is first, foremost, and always a working dog. Change any aspect of that, and you have lost the Pyr that we love for so many other reasons. It is maybe a very nice dog that we can appreciate, but not the unique ancient creature that comes to us from the cradle of civilization and is likely descended from the first dogs and certainly the first LGD of any breed. The Pyr worked as a team member. Traditionally for as long as we have any records, there was the shepherd, the Pyr (maybe several Pyrs) and the little dog, the

Dew Claws- Note they are rotated forward or anteriority from their normal position on the inside (medial side) of the foot in the picture.

Bergers (maybe several of them as well). The shepherd likely had some other herd animals such as goats and cows. This provided some food for everyone during the summer grazing periods in the mountains. It is troubling to this writer that in North America we place the Pyr out completely alone for long periods of time. I will produce an email from June of 2001. I will not identify its poster as that is not important, but it speaks volumes about how we expect extraordinary things from our Pyrs and how in the main they succeed admirably. Nevertheless, I think it is a problem for the breed in the long run as this is not what they did historically.

"Most people around here that have range dogs don't groom them. They get caught to get their vaccinations and that's about the extent of it. I have friends that run several thousand head of sheep on about 30,000 acres with quite a number of LGD's (Pyrs) and the dogs usually only see people a couple of times a year. They are completely in charge of the animals they guard. They are such magnificent animals and allow us to run stock where it would be virtually impossible without them."

This treatment of the Pyr is abuse. These ranchers must find a way to place a shepherd equivalent with the livestock. People for more than five thousand years have found a way and early on in the western states they brought shepherds from the Pyrenees Mountains. These were mostly Basque men who were not the oldest son in the family, and therefore, not entitled to any of the family estate.

Professor Will Monroe, the first President of the Great Pyrenees Club of America, shown with his dog, Basque of Basquaerie. Basque was out of the first litter born in America.

Breeding your Great Pyrenees

Pyrs had been around for about three thousand years in the year 5 BC.

Since this is an owner's handbook written more toward the new owner, any in-depth handling of this very complicated and multifaceted subject is beyond the scope of this book. The easy answer is, do not breed. There are many Pyrs available from excellent breeders and many more available from rescue. Truth is, we simply do not need any more bred. Now realizing that I very likely did not dissuade any of you who even casually want to breed, then I would counsel you to pursue the following course.

- Before trying to buy or procure a dog or bitch to breed, read more on breeding.

- Join the Great Pyrenees Club of America and study its ethical guidelines, paying close attention to the parts on breeding and breeders. This will be a resource for you to gain information about the breed.

- Devote time and personal resources toward the problem of rescue. The rescue problem is exploding everywhere, not just in Pyrs but all breeds. By doing this you will see the problem close up and see most likely why we do not need any more Pyrs.

- If all this has not convinced you otherwise, then find a mentor who is a member of the Great Pyrenees Club of America and convince them that you are a worthy student and someone who will do all you can to help the breed. Convince them that the breeding you do will somehow leave behind a positive influence instead of just more puppies and dogs for someone else to take care of, when you likely loose interest sometime in the next five years. Statistics tell us that ninety (90%) percent of people drop out of the dog world by five years. Those are pretty big odds that you will be one of the ninety percent, but your breeding issue will live ten to fourteen years.

Good luck. We need a few people who will work hard on behalf of the breed. Hopefully, breeding will be a minor part of the good things you bring to bear for the breed.

Monsieur Bernard Senac-Lagrange(1880-1954) is felt by many to be the greatest breed authority in the history of the breed.

Health Issues in the Great Pyrenees

A well-bred dog is very healthy. The breed generally is healthy as compared to some other breeds. There are some potentially serious health problems, however, the list is growing now as the popularity of the breed grows.

Skeletal Diseases

Being a large breed it is not surprising that many of the major problems of the breed revolve around this area, as it does many large and giant breeds.

Hip Dysplasia (HD)

Let's start with a success story. In North America we have identified (X-Rayed) and used disease free or acceptably free dogs with seemingly apparent success. We did this via dog specific identification and selection that I would hope we could apply to some other, really less complicated, problems. Dysplasia is a polygenetic problem seen in almost all dog breeds. Pyrs seem to have a lower incidence than many other large breeds in North America. The incidence in Europe is higher than in North America. I have no data to back this up, so take it solely as my impression. My simple answer to why we see less in North America is that we have worked on the problem for a long time and have been very serious about it. It takes many generations to see significant results, so the resolve needs to be long term and ongoing. We did it without genetic markers, we may have done some test breeding, but mostly we used disease free dogs in our breeding, and many breeders use disease free families of dogs in their breeding programs. A disease free dog with siblings (or parents, uncles, aunts, etc) who are affected can be just as bad as a dog that is affected. It has been described simply as an "abnormal formation of the hip socket; causes rear- limb lameness". It generally appears before two years of age. The condition can require surgery and can cause the dog much pain and disability. It can also be very painful, emotionally, for the owner and expensive financially. Some dogs with even a marked degree of Hip Dysplasia are totally asymptomatic and require no intervention. dysplastic dogs, or dogs that produce same should generally not be bred.

Luxation of the Patella

I am not sure how we are doing with this problem. My suspicion is that it is on the rise, primarily because of a high incidence in some very popular and active breeding programs that have enjoyed much success in the show ring. I have little to support this "impression". It does not look like we are identifying individual dogs and thus may be breeding them and their families.

In fairness, this is a complicated problem, charged with emotion, politics, etc. There has been a small improvement in the recognition of the problem, but some remain steadfast in their stonewalling of the problem, for what reasons one can only speculate.

Luxation of the patella is a polygenetic problem and it manifests itself under one year of age. This much seems clear. The problem is caused by poor development of the structures around the knee that hold the kneecap in place. The patella generally dislocates inward or medially, but in some cases it can dislocate outward or laterally. It can be a debilitating problem that many times requires surgery. It can cause much pain for the dog. It can also be heartbreaking and expensive for the owner of the dog. Some dogs with even a marked degree of luxation of the patella are totally asymptomatic and require no intervention. It seems that emulation of the success with Hip Dysplasia is the correct avenue to achieve success with this problem. Again, the problem may be more prevalent in Europe than in North America, but this is an impression of the author, nothing more. Dogs with luxation of the patella or those who produce it should not generally be bred.

Panosteitis

Panosteitis is a disease of the long bones in the legs of young dogs and bitches. It is primarily seen in the front legs but in more serious cases it will be seen in the rear legs as well. It will travel from leg to leg. It is a disease that is felt to be partially genetic, but its mode of inheritance in unknown. It is also thought to be associated with other factors such as diet, immunity, bacterial, and viral association. What we do know suggests strongly, a familial association with its incidence. It is generally seen before 18 months. In the past we usually observed the onset in our puppies at about 4 to six months. It usually lasts for a few weeks and is not a problem thereafter. There is a theory that a low fat, low protein diet will help the dog move through the bout quicker (less nutrition?). Our experience, and we tried the theory, is just the opposite. The dogs will eat very poorly when in pain from the disease anyway, and have marked malaise during the active symptom part of the disease under normal circumstances. A high quality, high nutrition diet is very desirable during this period of time. Stress, excitement, and activity are things to avoid. Except in the most painful cases we do not recommend any analgesic. Pyrs have an incredible tolerance for pain as it is and we want to limit the activity to prevent damage to the long bones.

On X-ray, the periosteum of the bone is enlarged and inflamed and presents as a "waffling pattern". Your vet, if familiar with the disease, will recognize this X-Ray pattern. It is this inflamed periosteum that can be injured during any period of exacerbation of the disease. Almost every case will pass without any residual effects, if one follows the advice of a high quality diet, rest, and elimination of all stress, including heat if possible. Stress can exacerbate the condition. In 2000 we rode a young bitch from Georgia to California to the GPCA National Specialty. This same bitch had never had the disease and had been shown extensively prior to this trip. She had two litter brothers who had the disease prior. She came out of the crate in California limping slightly and was not able to show. After returning to Georgia and a few days of rest at home, the limping disappeared. She continued her show schedule a few weeks later. This same bitch had a litter brother who had it in the rear legs as well as the front legs as a young dog. This young dog did not move correctly in the rear for a long period of time, and there was concern he might never move correctly. Fortunately this passed completely, and this young dog at about two years of age took first place in the American Bred Class at the 2001 Great Pyrenees Club of America National Specialty show held at Andover, Massachusetts. His movement was and continues to be excellent.

To repeat, generally the problem is confined to the front legs. Involvement in the rear legs is not a good sign and usually indicates, to this writer, that the involvement and course of the disease process will be more serious. After the active phase of the disease, it takes sometimes months before the dog or bitch achieves real normal status. This is more so with rear leg involvement. I would eliminate working dogs from their work during the active disease phase and give them time to return gradually. The disease can also come and go (wax and wane) over a few months period of time. This writer is, unfortunately, very experienced with this disease. Less so during the past five or six years since our breeding stock has shifted significantly and is now in a group of dogs with lower incidence.

It is very rare that the disease leaves any residual effects or lameness. Residual lameness, if it occurs, does improve over a period of years. We have only seen this in two dogs out of the 60 or so dogs we have observed with the condition in about 30 years of breeding.

Diagnoses is clinical and can involve the dog running a temperature, being lethargic, not eating, and the typical X-ray pattern mentioned above. In rare, extreme cases the dog will cry in pain and this is the time for some enteric-coated aspirin. Consult your vet on frequency of the analgesic.

In some cases, X-rays are not clear or are difficult to diagnose. One quick crude sign is to see if pressure from a thumbnail or blunt object pushed into the shaft of a long bone, such as the front leg, elicits any pain response. A word of caution, Pyrs have such a high pain tolerance I would not be fooled even with any apparent pain response. I would also limit the pressure I applied and would not let anyone else try very hard.

Hypertrophic Osteodystrophy (HOD)

Hypertrophic Osteodystrophy (HOD) is a developmental disease of young, rapidly growing large and giant-breed dogs. Dogs with HOD exhibit lameness in one or more limbs in association with swelling and inflammation of the growth plate areas (metaphyseal) regions of the long bones (arms and legs). The onset of clinical signs occurs generally before 8 months of age.

The dog exhibits mild pain to severe pain, fever, and loss of appetite. The prognosis can be very poor, but dogs can recover completely. Lameness varies in severity. The affected long- bone may be extremely swollen at the ends of the bones. Physical exam and history are use in making the diagnosis. Affected bones are warm and swollen on palpation. Fever of up to 106 degrees may be present. Loss of appetite, reluctance to move and weight loss may be noted. X-rays may show changes in the extremities- reflecting enlargement of the metaphysis. Typically, pain and swelling at the carpal area are classic diagnostic signs seen most frequently. Its mode of inheritance is unknown. The treatment is rest and control of pain symptoms, although some successful reports of antibiotics are seen in the literature.

I have never seen a case, although I was told of a case in one of the dogs we bred. It was not HOD, but Panosteitis we reviewed just above. This dog happened to be a litter brother of the two dogs I reference above under Panosteitis. The vet made the diagnosis with the admission that it was an "atypical case of HOD". It was Panosteitis classic and ran the course, as we would expect. I believe that the Vet and owner need to be very careful not to mistake the Panosteitis for HOD. In my opinion, the absence of the X-ray evidence of inflammation and swelling at the metaphysis would lead one to suspect Panosteitis. HOD seemed to involve the ends of long bones, where Panosteitis involves the shaft of the bone. Except in very severe cases, the outlook for Panosteitis is much better than for HOD. It is reported in the literature that dogs can return completely to normal from HOD.

My experience is that it is of extremely low incidence or non-existent in the breed. I would be very suspicious of any prior diagnoses without excellent X-ray and clinical diagnoses that are "right on point".

Osteochondritis Dissecans (OCD)

Osteochondritis Dissecans is seen in large dogs. In Pyrs and other large dogs we see it most commonly reported in the shoulders. It can occur in the elbows, hocks, or ankle/foot. I believe the shoulders are the major problem in the breed, but do not believe it is wide spread in Pyrs. We never see it in our breeding, and I seldom hear about it from others. A Pyr limping in the front, that is young, i.e. under two years old, but most commonly under one year of age, should be checked by a vet and Panosteitis ruled out. It generally occurs early during the growth phase of a young dog.

It can cause "loose bodies" sometimes called a "joint mouse" in the joint. It can lead to arthritis of the joint and can lead to serious problems in the joint. The mode of inheritance is not known. It is commonly suspected to be associated with diet, trauma, and other factors. It is felt by some to be at least partially familial in origin i.e. it runs in families more commonly than not.

It is felt in some very legitimate circles to be nutrition and trauma caused, possibly instead of or in addition to the genetic. Under the best of circumstances, it is a complicated problem that can be very serious. The condition in the elbows is termed Elbow Dysplasia.

It is diagnosed by your vet via X-ray, arthroscopy, history, and examination. Treatment varies from simple rest, to medication for pain and inflammation, all the way to surgery. The conservative recommendation as far as breeding is not to breed affected dogs or bitches. If you note a family with high incidence, it would be best to not breed any offspring from this family.

Chondrodysplasia (Dwarfism)

Few genetic diseases cause the furor or emotion that this one seems to generate. The condition known technically as Chondrodysplasia in Pyrs, involves multiple problems in the skeletal and vertebral system.

Diagnosis is definitive via x-ray as there are cases that are very mild and can be missed by the untrained observer or breeder. Dwarfism is caused by a simple recessive gene. It appears presently, that the affected Dwarfs are functionally sterile, as no successful breeding has been reported. Some breeding have been attempted, under even laboratory situations. The carrier animal is the problem and generates all the emotion when suddenly a litter with a dwarf or several dwarf pups pop up, seemingly out of nowhere from phenotypical normal parents.

In any affected dogs, the sire and dam both are carriers. The rub comes because the grandparents may have only one of them as carriers. So basically with a dwarf, one of the grandparents on both sides are carriers, but both may not be carriers.

As genetic problems go, this is a rather clear one. It is a simple recessive gene. The problem is identification of carriers, and that is where valid data is imperative. The Great Pyrenees Club of America has been working on this for years and are working with researchers who are making great strides, that we are told will benefit the breed fairly soon. That will be a great day. In the interim, it must be treated as any simple recessive problem.

Neurological Diseases

Except for Epilepsy and Spinal Muscular Atrophy, the breed is blessed mostly by the absence of these, generally, very serious problems.

Spinal Muscular Atrophy

In Pyrs, this condition seems to present itself late, i.e. after the sixth year of life. There is a chance it could be a type of spinal stenosis that is high enough in the spinal column to present symptoms in the front legs, but most likely it is a form of Spinal Muscular Atrophy. This is a central nervous system, degenerative process that is genetic. It is seen in many Pyrs and is widely ignored because it does not become very severe (noticeable) until many times into the 10th year or later in life. Mostly it is credited to being an old dog, but some dogs do not have it, so it is more.

The abnormal neurological reflexes in both the front and back legs are diagnostic of this type problem. They indicate an upper motor neuron lesion by their nature and presence. I suspect it begins earlier in life than we normally recognize it, maybe as early as the 5th or 6th year. It may subtly present itself in a stud dog, for example, beginning to have problems holding a bitch when breeding, as the back legs are clearly affected first and the most by diminished strength. There is probably a properceptive and sensory involvement as one of the characteristic signs of their gait is a "stomping", especially in the back legs. As the condition develops the toes can "curl" over (under) thus causing the dog to trip much easier. The less active a dog, the more the symptoms are evident. If an old dog goes down off their feet even for a day, the pathological reflexes are severe for them to overcome, i.e. the curling over of the toes in the front and back legs. Weight bearing inhibits these pathological reflexes. It is imperative that dogs with this condition be kept mobile in the upright weight bearing position. Weight bearing on all legs is essential to their well being and quality of life. When they get to the point that they are not able to get up from lying and are not able to re-achieve this status with some help and exercise (therapy), the end is very near. You will also see them not control fecal material, and it just seems to roll or "plop" out of them at any time. Frequently they will get up from lying and leave fecal material behind that comes out while lying.

Much of the above is based on my observing this in our dogs for 35 years and seeing the same in many other dogs over the same period of time. I had several dogs examined in the early days, when the pathological reflexes were noted to me, and it was described as I earlier delineated it above. My experience is that it takes years once you start noticing it in your dog, and your dog appears fine otherwise. There does not appear to be any apparent pain or discomfort, just slowly increased weakness more noticeable in the back legs-- a very characteristic "stomping" gait, and the stool problems are seen later. Once you have seen the gait, you will not forget it, as it is very distinctive.

As far as breeding, most, if not all the get, is on the ground when the condition is diagnosed. Fortunately, the dog seems to live a fairly normal life to that point and most of the remaining years thereafter. I have wondered about the many dogs I have placed in working environments but have not received any negative reports. I suspect when the dog begins looking like an old dog, the owners start making accommodations for him or her and chalk it up to "old age". That is what most of us do anyway. It is surprising what some of these old dogs can do anyway.

Epilepsy

Epilepsy has been around a long time, but it seemed to be very rare until recently in North America. Again this increase (if it is one) seems tied to the success of a few active breeders in winning the shows and selling puppies. It is reported to be a recessive trait of undetermined mode of transmission. We probably do not really know if it is recessive, dominant, or some variant. It is reported as occuring at over one year and this is what is seen in Pyrs. It is common to see dogs and bitches showing the first signs at two to three years old. This is especially true of bitches. What this means is, if the breeder is hiding the problem, chances are you might have bred your dog or bitch at least one time before you diagnose the problem.

I was amused and bemused by a situation in a breed rare in North America that had and still has a very high incidence of Epilepsy. Most of the import stock (really 100%) was from one breeder in Europe. When this European breeder was asked about the incidence of Epilepsy in those dogs sold and exported to North America, who were epileptic and were breeding epileptic get in large percentages, the response was that this was "a North American problem". That is the way not to solve a genetic problem. Without a mode of inheritance known, we have to identify individual dogs and families of dogs affected and carefully not use these dogs going forward. Not using even some potentially affected dogs, with all parties aware and consciously monitoring the offspring, is much preferable and will, I predict, lead to more success than the hiding and continued breeding of these affected dogs. Identification and selection are the keys here once again.

If you have a dog that is epileptic, it can be controlled by medication much of the time. These dogs should not be bred. Dogs that produce it should not be bred anymore as well.

Eye Problems

So far we have identified Progressive Retinal Atrophy, Juvenile Cataracts, Geriatric Cataracts, Persistent Pupillary Membranes (Iris-Cornea), Multifocal Retinopathy, Retinal Detachment, Optic

Nerve Hypoplasia, Distichiasis, and Entropion in Pyrs in North America.

Multifocal Retinopathy (MR)

Some would argue this is not a disease because it is reported in some people's hands as being functionally asymptomatic. The huge problem with dogs' eyesight is designing a functional test with any validity or significance. We cannot eye test dogs. Clinically, from an eye examination perspective, there is a lot going on in this disease. Even those who say that functionally it does not cause the dog any problems will say very quickly that it should not become like the Collie Eye Anomaly (CEA), i.e., seen in all or almost all the dogs of the breed. When the vet ophthalmologist sees the amount of pathology in the visual fields as they do in MR, why would we want our dogs working with visual field impairments? In addition, there are owners who are adamant that there are visual field impairments that manifest themselves in functional problems. They talk about the dog "running with its head close to the ground" as symptomatic of this problem. Lets use common sense here, dogs working in low light conditions do not need to be handicapped by visual field impairments.

MR involves detachment of the retina that forms lesions, i.e. blind spots in the vision. No debate about this. The debate is do these blind spots impair the dog's functional vision? Some say yes and some say no. Those who say no believe because a dog can complete a maze, its vision is not affected. Others say the vision is affected, and completing the maze did not measure the difficulty the dog had with the maze caused by the vision impairment. A working dog must do more than run a maze and that is the rub. Our dogs must aspire to be more than our pets, lab rats, and companions or we will have changed the breed forever. We know the brain is able in humans to compensate for blind spots in the visual field, but I don't think any of us want to put our visually impaired dogs out to work at night, twilight, or dawn conditions without excellent eyesight. Their job is tough enough already, and the consequences are pretty severe if they fail and are killed by a predator or group of predators.

To this writer this seems pretty simple. Since our eye specialists know there is visual field "blind spots" caused by the detachment of the retina, this is a problem we do not want in the breed. It is felt by at least one researcher who is a canine ophthalmologist, to be a simple recessive disorder. That presents with it the very large problem of the "carriers" going generations without producing pathology. On top of all that, if Pyrs were not examined, how would one ever know the degree of the disease? It presents itself early, at between 11 and 20 weeks. If nothing else, it would be detected if your Pyr's eyes were examined at six months of age. If it is not present then, it will not appear. There is some suggestion that it is seen with PPM, but I do not see anything clear to that point, at least now. No treatment is available.

Juvenile Cataracts

This is also termed developmental cataracts and late onset cataracts. One should distinguish this from congenital cataracts that occurs very early in age, i.e. the first few weeks of life, at birth, or even developed prior to whelping; and geriatric cataracts, which occurs late in life at eight or more years give or take a year or so. Juvenile cataracts is also seen in the literature as early onset and progressive cataracts. Its onset is from birth to six years of age but generally after two months, but commonly even later and up to 4 or 5 years of age. Senile or geriatric cataracts is seen in old age of the dog and the etiology is not really known.

Juvenile cataracts is the one that the breed needs to pay particular attention. To further complicate the problem, cataracts can be caused by problems other than heredity; but one must clearly understand that unless you can clearly identify a non-hereditary causation, one must assume the cause to be hereditary. Age of onset is diagnostic, as many will develop between 6 months and 2 years of age. Yearly rechecks are recommended until the dog is 6 years of age. Most breeders will find it hard to check all their dogs yearly, so I would recommend that a dog or bitch be checked before it is bred. If clear, it should be checked again within a couple years of the initial check. I would examine all dogs at about 2 years of age. In the case of a young stud, you might check him as early as one year, and I would repeat then at two years or before he turns three. In Pyrs, the genetics appears to likely be a simple recessive mode of inheritance. At least, it is assumed to most likely be that. Early onset cataracts are generally seen under three years of age.

Early onset cataracts rarely lead to blindness. In fact it can be very minor. It is characterized by an opacity or cloudiness in the lens. This is one of those good news, bad news situations. The condition generally is not very debilitating to the pet and companion Pyr but can be. We do not want juvenile cataracts, like CEA in Collies, we mentioned earlier, as well. To do so might leave the dogs unable to work and would be playing Russian roulette on which dogs would have the more profound symptoms that result in blindness. There is always the possibility that high incidences of the problem would lead to a strain that was much more serious, and the breed would have nowhere to go to clear itself. It needs to stop right where it is now.

Surgery is indicated in advanced cases Fortunately, most of our contemporary dogs in our homes seem normal except at eye examination. I am not sure this would be the case at all if the dog had to work for a living, and the breed must be able to work

.

Persistent Pupillary Membranes (PPM)

Persistent Pupillary Membranes (PPM) seems mostly benign in Pyrs, but there is a small class that can be a problem. In fact PPM's are not uncommon on eye exam. The PPM is the remnant of a prenatal developmental growth involving the eyes. Basically, the membrane is not fully absorbed at birth and in the first five weeks of life as it does normally. Most of these are Iris-to-Iris PPM's. The Iris to cornea PPM's are problematical. These PPM's cause opacities (cataracts) at the point they are attached to the lens capsule. The Iris to Cornea PPM's also causes opacities in the cornea. These can be small or large depending on the severity of the degree of PPM's. These can improve or resolve somewhat with age, but the more severe cases are a problem. Fortunately these two problem classes of PPM are not common. CERF says the Iris-to-Iris PPM is "breeders option" as far as breeding. The Iris to Cornea or the Iris to Lens PPM's should not be bred. The mode of inheritance is not known and the age of onset is under three months.

Entropion

Entropion used to be the only eye disorder anyone was every concerned with in Pyrs. It was identified by Edith and Seaver Smith in their dogs at Quibbletown, and essentially bred out of these same dogs. One will occasionally see this condition or hear of one along the way. This is a condition that causes the eyelid to roll inward causing damage to the eye from the lashes rubbing against the eye. The mode of inheritance has not been determined. It can be diagnosed under one year of age. Surgery is the treatment or correction. Since the mode of inheritance is not known, it is wise to eliminate those dogs and bitches from your breeding program that have produced the problem, and certainly never breed an affected dog or bitch.

Distichiasis

Distichiasis is the abnormal growth of an eyelash(es) from the meibomian glands along the eyelid margin. This positions them directly out of the lid margin, and they can come in contact with the eye surface. Untreated, distichiasis can lead to corneal ulcers, chronic eye pain, excessive tearing, and eyelid spasms. It is almost certainly uncomfortable for the dog and permanent removal of the offending eyelashes is best when any clinical signs are present.

Surgery is the treatment. It is reported to from undetermined mode of inheritance. It usually shows up at less than six months of age. Elimination of affected dogs and bitches from the breeding program is recommended.

To my knowledge this condition has been reported very few times. At best, this condition would be painful and cause eye damage to affected dogs unless diagnosed and treated. Surgery for correction might be expensive.

Optic Nerve Hypoplasia

Optic Nerve Hypoplasia is an undersized nerve that is noted where it enters the eyeball. It impairs vision and in extreme cases can cause blindness. The pupil of affected eye(s) may be dilated. The mode of inheritance is undetermined. The age of onset is under 3 months. No treatment is warranted. Affected dogs should be eliminated from breeding programs.

Again, like above, to my knowledge, this condition has been heretofore not described in the Pyr. Any condition that produces blindness should be taken extremely seriously.

Retinal Detachment

Also seen as Primary Retinal Detachment. Its mode of inheritance is undetermined and the age of onset varies. If in one eye only, the other eye may be normal. If bilateral, blindness can occur. Some sources seem to suggest this may be (at times at least) a very serious Retinal dysplasia. In the severe form of dysplasia, the 2 retinal layers do not come together at all and retinal detachment occurs. It can occur due to trauma or other conditions including surgery, specifically cataract surgery. Sometimes surgery to reattach the retina is indicated.

Dogs have such good "other" senses, they adapt to familiar surroundings to a remarkable degree. So a family dog may go undiagnosed. Clearly these dogs cannot be expected to work and again not working changes the breed from the core of its essence. I would not breed a dog with this condition unless I could clearly identify another cause, and then surgery might offer a correction. I am not sure surgery offers a correction with a long-standing hereditary problem, as it looks like time is of the essence in the surgery after onset. At best, surgery would be expensive and not always successful, or fully successful.

Endocrine Diseases

Addisons Disease - Primary Hypoadrenocorticism

We are seeing more and more of this disease in the past few years. Addisons Disease is also termed Primary Hypoadrenocorticism. The genetic mode of transmission is undetermined. Onset is before five years generally. Clinically the dog shows poor appetite, vomiting and lethargy. The condition has periods of exacerbation and seeming remission. There can be tremor, weight loss, and diarrhea. Symptoms can lead to hypothermia, weakness, and collapse. It is more frequent in a middle aged female dog, but can be seen at any age and either sex. It is thought to be an "autoimmune" related disease. Once diagnosed, it can be treated very successfully by your vet with medication. I would not recommend breeding an affected dog or bitch for several reasons, one being the genetic potential of moving the problem to future generations. We need to know more about this condition. It has been reported it in Pyrs.

Hypothyroidism

This problem is being reported more in the breed. It is reported as being propagated both recessive and unknown (idiopathic form). Onset date is generally less than 2 years of age, but the idiopathic form can be seen up to five years of age. The Oxford Labs state that dogs can develop this anytime in life, especially if it is Autoimmune Thyroiditis (TgAA) origins. The test for TgAA (Autoimmune Thyroiditis) will diagnose this problem up to two years before any clinical signs appear. Tests are not expensive. Breeding stock should be screened for this problem. Because the test is easily accomplished, those dogs with the recessive gene can be reduced and hopefully eliminated.

You see many dogs with low normal or borderline thyroid studies that may be affected as well. These seem to be connected with irregular heat cycles in bitches, possibly Uterine inertia in these same bitches, as well as the classic problems of coat and skin problems, poor appetite, weight loss, etc. A skinny dog or bitch with poor coat would beg for this to be ruled out. Sometimes a Pyr with even a low normal value on the Thyroid test would benefit from a low level of treatment.

It is possibly from an autoimmune connection of Hypothyroidism (Autoimmune Thyroiditis) as well as the idiopathic. The Oxford Labs who notes that the OFA maintains a registry for the disease states that the idiopathic form is many times just the end stage of the Autoimmune Thyroiditis. They note that Autoimmune Thyroiditis is the most common cause of hypothyroidism. Affected dogs are easily and successfully treated with L-thyroxine (T4) tablets. The cost is not great.

123

Should these dogs be bred? There is debate over this, but probably not. Many of us do, but I think we should evaluate carefully what we are doing. Some feel this is a rapidly growing problem in the breed and that being said, could become very serious in years to come. Breeders need to look carefully at their dogs and try to make breeding decisions that lessen the likelihood of this genetic problem going to the next generation.

Urinary System Diseases

Juvenile Renal Disease

This is sometimes referred to as Juvenile Kidneys and Renal Dysplasia. It is a simple recessive, genetic disorder that is not sex linked. It occurs mostly before one year of age. It is observed in at least 20 other breeds besides the Great Pyrenees. It is a serious disease that more frequently than not results in death. Affected animals will rarely be bred before the occurrence of the disease. The real problem, genetically, are the carriers in the breed. It should be approached like all simple recessive disorders. That involves information on affected dogs and carriers. Eliminating carriers from a breeding program is necessary.

Heart and Vascular Diseases

Subarotic Stenosis (SAS

This is a very serious, genetic related disease whose mode of transmission is not fully understood. It is being reported in the breed in North America in just the last ten years or so. It is thought to be both dominant and recessive, plus associated with other modifying genetic factors. It is polygenetic and occurs before one year of age. It causes a narrowing at the base of the aorta as a result of a fibrous band, causing murmurs, weakness and sudden death. The disease is seen in Newfoundland Dogs and is a serious problem in that breed, as well as several others. Mild cases can be difficult to diagnose, and diagnoses can be expensive involving sophisticated cardiac examinations and procedures. Likewise, screening dogs in affected lines can be very expensive and not always reliable. Any occurrence of the disease in a dog will generally result in problems being passed to offspring of the single affected parent. This indicates a strong dominant genetic component to the genetic transmission of the disease. All dogs that are confirmed to have any degree of the disease must be eliminated from a breeding program. Get from a breeding where it is felt that at least one parent was the contributor of the genetic makeup of the problem for the disease, should be carefully evaluated. The get should be several years old before they are bred and cleared by a vet who is a Diplomat of the American College of Veterinary Internal Medicine, specializing in cardiology or the equivalent in the country that you reside.

Murmur

Murmurs are caused by several problems, so are likely the result of some other heart problems that we should not speculate upon. Sometimes they are not serious and other times they are depending on the underlying causation. You need diagnosis and proper work up to know what is going on.

Heart Valve Problems

This category needs more definition. I suspect it involves the mitral, and the tricuspid valves of the heart. Both problems are classified as undetermined mode of inheritance and onset at about one year or less. They usually show up from two years to seven years of age.

Pulmonic stenosis

Narrowing of the pulmonic artery where it attaches to the heart is the location of this problem, causing murmurs and enlargement of the right side of the heart. This is classified as polygenetic mode of inheritance and onset at one year or less. No range of onsets ages specified. Affected dogs and bitches should not be bred. We need to learn more about this condition.

Cardiomyopathy

Abnormality of the heat muscle may cause edema of the lung, weakness at exercise, and sudden death. The mode of inheritance is polygenetic and usually shows up at 2 years or less. Affected dogs and bitches should not be bred. We need to learn more about this condition.

Hematopoietic & Lymphatic Diseases

Hemophilia

This is a sex linked, recessive gene present at birth. It involves a blood clotting deficiency condition and can result in death to the affected dog. Affected dogs should not be bred and familial links should be carefully considered if there is any family history of the condition, before using any descendant or relative.

Von Willebrand's Disease (vWD

This is a condition of the blood that has a reduced factor VIII in the blood (vWF), resulting in a prolonged bleeding time. It is not a disease in the classic sense, but a genetic disorder that is not uncommon in dogs. The condition may be mild, moderate, or severe and can cause death. It is both recessive and incomplete dominance mode of inheritance in three types. It usually shows up within the first year of life. It is described as a common, usually mild bleeding disorder in people and in dogs. It occurs in both dogs and bitches.

There are three types, the most common being Type I, thought to be autosomal trait with incomplete dominance. This means that the offspring can inherit the disorder if either parent carries (only one parent) the gene, but not all offspring will be affected to the same extent. Type I is known in the literature to occur "widespread" in Doberman Pinscher's and is also relatively common in the Scottish Terrier and Shetland Sheepdog population. There is an increased risk in the Golden Retriever, Standard and Miniature Poodle, Welsh Pembroke Corgi, Miniature Schnauzer, Basset Hound, German Shepherd, Rottweilers, Manchester Terrier, Keeshond, and Standard and Miniature Dachshund. Get that inherit the Type I vWD from both parents (homozygotes) die before birth or shortly thereafter.

This condition occurs in most breeds and in mixed-breed dogs as well. I suspect this data has never been developed in the breed other than casually and certainly has not been studied by anyone that this author is aware.

Type II vWD is rare. It is autosomal recessive. Type III vWD is very rare. It is an autosomal recessive trait. So, it is most "likely" we are talking about Type I that affects Pyrs.

Affected animals should not be bred, and careful study of the relatives should be considered before breeding them as well due to the complex genetic mode of transmission. This is a serious genetic problem for the dog, the breeder, and potentially the breed as a whole. The potential mode of inheritance could be very troubling if it became very common at all.

Carriers of the trait can be predicted by a test that measures the vWF level. A reduced level of vWF (25 to 60 per cent) without bleeding problems is diagnostic. Those with these reduced vWF levels can be confirmed by test breeding stock. Affected and carrier dogs and bitches should not be bred.

Liver and Pancreas

The breed seems in fairly good shape in this area. I do not believe Diabetes is a very great problem in the breed

Diabetes Mellitus

Diabetes Mellitus is a genetic inherited condition that has a mode of inheritance of recessive undetermined with an onset date of three years or younger.

It is characterized by excessive sugar accumulating in the blood and urine due to a lack of, or inability to use insulin. Diabetes can be treated with diet, exercise, and medication. Pyrs affected should not be bred and bitches might have problems with the metabolism necessary to whelp and nurse puppies.

Alimentary Diseases

Except for Bloat, this area is not generally a problem of the breed. Bloat is not a big problem in certain breeding lines.

Bloat

Bloat, known accurately as Bloat and Gastric Torsion and Gastric Dilatation-Volvulus involves distention and twisting of the stomach, resulting in discomfort, vomiting, and ineffectual retching. The twisting of the stomach cuts off the blood supply to the stomach, causing the death of the stomach tissue. Death of the dog is common. Its mode of inheritance is undetermined. If it occurs, it generally occurs under seven years of age. This is a very serious problem. Fortunately, it is not common in Pyrs. Getting to a vet quickly is important should you ever suspect this to be occurring.

Even treated dogs have a mortality of 35%. Treatment many times involves surgery with stitching the stomach to the abdominal wall to prevent it from becoming twisted again. Once the stomach bloats and becomes twisted on itself, cutting of the blood supply to the stomach, it will reoccur easier the next time if not prevented.

Reproductive Diseases

I believe the breed is in good condition in this area as well, but anecdotally I seem to hear of more conception problems, whelping problems, and nursing problems. This area needs to be observed closely in the future.

Uterine Inertia (UI)

Uterine Inertia falls under the heading of Dystocia that is generally, difficulty whelping puppies. Uterine Inertia is one of the causes of Dystocia. There is primary UI and secondary UI. Secondary UI occurs later in the process and seems probable that it is a fatigue disorder. Primary occurs in the first stage of labor and although it has several degrees of how it affects the process, it might be hormonal based. Our experience is that when a bitch has this problem, she will have it in every pregnancy. The older she is, the more advanced will be the problem. There is no real evidence I can discover to indicate it is linked genetically, but one has to consider any hormone problem as having some likely genetic disposition between generations.

In a discussion held with Judy Cooper of Tip 'N Chip Kennels about UI and it being genetic, she and I both fully agreed that, in our opinion, it is genetic. If the dam had it, there was a greatly increased likelihood that the bitch puppy get of that dam would also have it. I have no feeling at all about probability of the male puppies producing increased incidence in their bitch get puppies. There is no documentation here except from two breeders, one having bred since 1947 in their family and myself since 1972.

I would listen to the old breeders here and they will always tell you that you should use good healthy bitches that have no, or few problems whelping and nursing puppies. They believe, as does this writer, that there is a general link between problem bitches with any conception, whelping, or nursing problems. Most, if not all, of a breeder's problems can be minimized by using bitches that have no problems in the family lines i.e. mother, grandmother, etc.

Cancers

There is growing evidence that many forms of cancers are genetically linked although not always heritable. This is a complex question that is just now in the cutting edge stages of research. See the information below on Osteosarcoma. Much of it may apply to many cancers, especially the loss of genes that actually suppress to formation of cancers.

Bone Cancer

Osteosarcoma

Osteosarcoma is an aggressive form of cancer that is the dread of every Pyr owner. The prognosis is very poor. The incidence in the breed does not appear to be great, or I should say, my

Leah with her favorite senior Vet student Cameron at one of her post-op amputation check ups. It was interesting to see Leah show her cute personality right from the start to the Veterinary doctors and students.

experience with the dogs we have bred for 30 years, is almost non-existent. We do hear more than we would like to hear of it being a problem, so maybe we have just been blessed, or have a line that is not prone to the problem. This last line of reasoning seems to suggest some genetic link. There is not very much in the lay literature relative this condition and its genetic basis if any. It is not listed in one prominent book on Canine Genetic Diseases.

There is evidence that large breeds have a much higher incidence of osteosarcoma. Tall seems to be more important than heavy. Males have a higher incidence than females. Intact males seem to have a lower incidence than neutered males. These last two figures are for dogs in general and not Pyr specific. In the large breeds some breeds, seem to have a higher incidence. This again suggests some genetic component to the occurrence of the problem, but other factors at present seem to get the nod over genetics as a causative factor. Still, one has to critically consider the possibility, when you see a good friend loose three very beloved littermates just months apart from Bone Cancer. Anecdotal? You bet, but we need to at least consider these things because the odds are very steep that this would happen. It appears we have a lot more to learn about this condition, especially as it may or may not relate to genetics.

Some extremely interesting information just came available from a major research project on bone cancer in dogs that focused on large, tall dogs. I will list some of the important observations below.

There are mutations of specific genes that increase the probability or risk that an individual will develop a tumor (actually that a cell will become transformed and give rise to a tumor). It is clear now that cancer is a genetic disease, although it is not always heritable.

There is little information regarding the identity of genes associated with heritable or sporadic (non-heritable) canine cancers.

Investigation of cancer susceptibility in families or breeds of dogs is of critical importance to dog breeders and dog owners alike. Unlike other heritable conditions, genetic susceptibility to cancer may not manifest in disease until a dog has reached middle age, and long after it has achieved breeding potential.

In the case of bone tumors, large and giant breed- dogs are at greater risk to develop appendicular osteosarcoma, due to the greater number of cell divisions that occur in the growth plates to achieve proper bone length. Additional heritable factors are likely to play a role (at least one family of dogs was shown to share such a genetic characteristic, although the precise genetic factor remains undefined). In addition there may be epigenetic factors (those that control responses to the environment, or genes that do not participate in carcinogenesis directly, but rather they control the activity of select oncogenes or tumor suppressor genes) that similarly add to increased cancer risk.

Hearing and Balance

I do not believe this area is a problem very much at all. I have never known or seen a dog I knew was hearing impaired or deaf (outside Dwarfism complex). A few have been reported, so I present the below information.

Deafness

"Deafness-not further defined" is several problems lumped into this category. So the mode of inheritance is almost everything. One prominent expert on Canine Genetic disorders states the condition will be evident by 6 months or less.

I would think that any diagnosed cases of deafness be examined closer to try to identify the type problem, if possible. A very old dog such as the 15 year old I would not even report, but certainly the 1 year old onset is something to consider as far as its genetic basis and future breeding, as will its familial relationship to the problem. We do know that Dwarfs have deafness and/or hearing difficulties. Hearing impaired or deaf dogs cannot work effectively, or maybe I should say, would have much more difficulty working because of a loss or impairment of a keen sense they depend on normally. They can be happy and well-adjusted pets and companions.

C. Seaver and Edith K. Smith at Quibbletown circa 1974. Pictured with Ch. Quibbletown Jim Dandy

Behavioral Diseases

Actually I believe this area has improved a lot in the past 20 years. I see less shy, timid, or aggressive dogs than I did just a few years ago.

Excessive Aggressiveness

Classified as attacking or biting without reasonable provocation. The mode of Inheritance is undetermined and it occurs around 3 years old but also in younger and older Pyrs. This is not normal Pyr behavior. The Pyr that bites unprovoked and/or bites any family member has either a major temperament problem, or some medical problem such as a brain tumor, etc. Young dogs can "mouth" and this is not abnormal, but should be stopped before any pattern is established past this young puppy or dog stage of life. Anything that continues past these young stages of life is clearly abnormal for the breed and cannot be tolerated.

Most of your experienced breeders know from long experience that temperament, both good and bad, are highly heritable. I never recommend breeding any dog that has an aggressive, timid, or fear problem. You will get the same in the get, almost certainly. These dogs must be eliminated completely from all breeding programs. Do not confuse this with dog on dog aggression. While this may seem abnormal, and it is at times embarrassing and unpleasant to observe, it may be very normal dog behavior and have to do with the canine hierarchy. If you have a highly aggressive Pyr toward other dogs, you need to work with him to develop social manners and make sure the dog knows this is not appropriate, unless there is some real threat. The Pyr is to too large and potentially dangerous a dog to perpetuate these genetic problems.

Rage

Episodic Dyscontrol Syndrome

This condition has been reported anecdotally in the breed. Its mode of inheritance is undetermined and age of onset is 3 years of age or before. It occurs most commonly in males and is characterized by unprovoked or minimally provoked attacks.

My understanding of this condition is that it is very dangerous to dogs, and people. These dogs should never be bred, as the danger to future generations is too great. I believe it almost never occurs in the breed, and we need to keep it that way.

Megaesophagus

Megaesophagus is the most common cause for regurgitation in the dog. Regurgitation results from the inability of the esophagus to contract properly and propagate the food to the stomach. As a result, the ingested food and/or liquid remains in the esophagus, for anywhere from minutes to much longer. The food not arriving to the stomach causes the full sensation; the dog will continue to eat. As a result, the esophagus often enlarges as it dilates greatly with food, hence the name of the disease. Most cases have no apparent cause, and are therefore given the name, idiopathic megaesophagus. Some cases are caused secondary to underlying disease, namely hypothyroidism or myasthenia gravis and are thus called acquired secondary megaesophagus.

A very rare congenital disease, called a vascular ring anomaly is also possible, but these are usually seen only in very young puppies. The typical age of onset of canine megaesophagus is 7 - 15 years of age according to many sources. Clinical signs of megaesophagus will vary depending on severity and may include: regurgitation from minutes to several hours after eating or drinking, excessive salivation, mild to moderate weight loss, coughing, or wheezes. Some dogs experience pneumonia, secondary to aspiration of regurgitated contents. This is perhaps the most dangerous consequence of the disease.

The diagnostic work-up for megaesophagus begins with chest x-rays. The x-rays may show the esophagus dilated with food and will determine whether or not there is secondary aspiration pneumonia. In some cases, the nature of the ingested material does not allow for visualization of a dilated esophagus. If the history fits megaesophagus, but a dilated esophagus is not seen on routine x-rays, then a contrast study can be performed, where prior to the x-ray, a radio-opaque liquid is swallowed.

Your Vet will diagnose and treat the condition. One simple thing you can do is elevate the food dish to or just above stomach level.

Food Allergies

I am separating food allergies from other allergies, but many times they occur in some combination. This makes the diagnostic problem quite complicated and requires the handling of a skilled professional who specializes in the area.

The problem has become epidemic. It is seen in many degrees of involvement from very mild to severe. While there are atypical cases and cases complicated by other allergies such as contact and airborne, there are some simple and consistent symptoms you and your Vet should be on the lookout.

- Feet licking. In your Pyr the feet will be red from constant licking
- Shaking the head frequently which is probably indicative of ear irritation.
- Hot spot formation. Probably the result of skin irritations secondary to staff infection.

- Redness or erythema of the skin, many times associated with skin eruptions.

Often all the symptoms above will be present, but are minor in nature.

There is no simple explanation for the cause of the problem. It is said to be heritable, but they cannot reproduce it in any breeding, so it's a very complicated problem likely aggravated by food, environment, and lifestyle. Having been around as long as I have, I think there has been a dramatic increase in its occurrence. I see this also in all breeds as we have a boarding kennel and see more in all dogs it seems.

I believe the food we feed is a great contributor to the incidence of skin problems. Over a long time period the immune system that combats such problems become fatigued and less effective in dealing with the problem, plus the system ages and operates less effective. Consequently the problems become more evident as the dog ages, plus a build up of toxins in the system is likely as well.

Skin is an organ. It's at the end of the line so to speak. It can be slow to show symptoms and last to respond to any treatment especially medication. Ears are included here also, but have their own little peculiarities. They are also at the end of the line. In addition because the ears on Pyrs are down the ear canal holds moisture and is a prime place to develop yeast. Ear mites complicate the problem. So you have three problems in ears-yeast, mites, and bacterial infections and all three have to be addressed plus the food allergy itself. In addition, it is not uncommon that other allergies can contribute such as airborne agents.

My answer to the food allergy is an "elimination diet" started at any signs of what may be food allergies. If you are lucky you may only have to go through one course of antibiotics to clear the secondary staph skin infections. There can be yeast secondary as is seen in the ears. A good bath or two with antifungal shampoo is also indicated. Then an alternate protein food with NO Chicken or beef is indicated. Lamb being a popular diet lately is being added to the list, so maybe no lamb as well. Lamb has been the alternate protein of choice, but that is changing. There are single protein, single carbohydrate diets out now that are grain free. Some of them are also human grade food. For more information of feeding see that section. Basically I like to rotate the food between as many alternate proteins as I can reasonably find and keep on hand. You can do this yourself and the only cost, after the initial treatment by the Vet for the secondary problems, is the food. You must be vigilant. You have to know every treat or scrap the dog eats. One mishap can trigger the process. It is a very unforgiving scenario. Read all the ingredients carefully, not just the first five. No chicken, beef, and maybe lamb anywhere in the ingredients list.

Poultry fat is considered chicken. Turkey can have poultry added. Read carefully.

Activities with you and your Pyr

Skijourning

This is an activity in snow where the dog or dogs, in this case a Pyr pulls a skier. Looks like a lot of fun and may have a functional component in cross-country snow travel. There are companies who specialize in the equipment necessary for the dog.

Backpacking

For camping, walking, or cross-country travel, the Pyr has always been a very willing backpacker. You can buy the backpack from many providers.

Hiking

Same as above, but with or without the backpack. I always think when I hear about a person, especially a woman, being kidnapped and harmed while in rural areas that chances are the company of a Pyr would have prevented this from ever occurring. The dog will love the activity and time with you. Off lead may be a challenge as the breed may decide to go off to check it out. It may not be appreciated by the parties they check out very much, so one needs to make sure either the dog reliably comes when called (good obedience training) or use a flexi lead or similar.

Carting

This has become a dog activity in some shows. There are various activities from weight pulling, to simple carting, to pulling people. Carts and apparatus can be found and purchased from several places. Sledding would fall under this category as well.

Dog show activities

There is a lot to do here. There is confirmation, obedience,

agility, and now rally activities that are formalized activities under AKC. All are very popular and can be quite enjoyable for you and your Pyr. If

It takes a talented pair to make this pretty picture.
My son Gaelen Gentzel showing Mordecai.

you choose obedience, be prepared with tons of patience and a very good sense of humor.

Therapy dogs

It is not surprising that Pyrs are so good in this setting as they have such a nurturing nature. Therapists sometimes use Pyrs with clients, especially children, handicapped or mentally challenged.

Hospital and Nursing Home visitation

There is a small army of dogs who work in hospitals, nursing homes, and other settings for the benefit of the patients and residents. It is simply the therapeutic presence of the Pyr, and is very popular and helpful in all the settings. You can contact the Delta Society, 875 - 124th Ave NE #101, Bellevue, WA 98005. www.deltasociety.org for more information on how to get your dog in this activity.

Knitting

Sweater hair knitted from Pyr.

You can save the hair from your Pyr's coat. Have it made into yarn and then you can knit the hair into garments, dolls, etc. Pictured is Anna Kivimaki wearing a sweater knitted from the hair of the dog she is holding, Bazen de Soum. Bazen was the first dog imported into the USA circa 1930's. The hair is very warm and makes attractive garments, etc.

Sledding

Pyrs are eager sled dogs. They are not noted for their speed, but strength and endurance is something that can recommend the Pyr in this activity. Pictured in harness with a couple other dogs is

Pyr in harness for sledding circa 1930's

Bazen de Soum again. Picture was on an occasion of Anna Kivimaki making a cross county trip circa mid 1930's. The over eighty-mile trip was in extreme weather in Newfoundland.

Where should I buy a good Pyr?

The obvious answer is from a reputable breeder, but how will you know if they are reputable? Breeders who are members of the Great Pyrenees Club of America (GPCA) subscribe to a code of ethics. That is a good start. Here are some clues beyond that. In my opinion, the following guidelines would be a tip off to a good breeder.

- They give a lifetime guarantee on the dog.

- They clear and make public the results of tests for genetic problems like hip dysplasia, and luxating patella. Don't be put off here by some off handed dismissal of the question. A serious breeder will fully answer the question and supply the information you are asking for. The two conditions listed are a bare minimum.

- They give a no questions asked, lifetime return policy on the dog. In fact, many will require the return to them of the Pyr. They likely will not return your money, but will want the dog back with them.

There are some good working breeders who do not belong to GPCA but there are so many more that are not good honest breeders. The old axiom Caveat Emptor (Buyer Beware) applies here to the maximum.

How about rescue? Yes, but do your homework and find a good rescue organization. Understand the inherent problems in some rescue dogs. There are many great, needy, special dogs just waiting for you to come and give them their forever home. In return they will forever love and protect you and your flocks. If it does not work out, rescue will help you with the next step, but be determined for it to work out. Your dog needs not to be bounced around any more and hopefully rescue has screened out the problem dogs. That is one reason to find a reputable rescue organization to seek your Pyr.

Good luck. Unless you are going for a rescue dog, buy the  breeder not the puppy. That means don't expect to find the puppy just the minute you want it. One of the signs of maturity is delayed gratification. That doubly applies here. Your Pyr will live 12-14 years, hopefully. It's a big decision. A year or more wait on the right breeder is normal. You want that special dog, so be prepared to wait and invest the time doing so in the decision.

If you need a working dog, see the special section on the Pyr as a livestock guardian dog. In the section that follows that working dog section I have taken the AKC standard for the breed and selected important provisions of that standard that describes the ideal Great Pyrenees, which is synonymous with the ideal working dog for your livestock. You should see in reading that section that the standard for the breed is not just some description of the beauty aspects of the breed, but how they relate to the dogs ability and effectiveness in working with your livestock. This is another reason to buy from a breeder who breeds to the standard even if they have no understanding or appreciation for what you need or what is required of the breed in working.

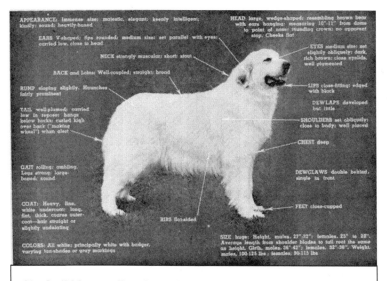

Ch. Quibbletown Dutchess. Used as an ideal standard visualization subject. She was considered by many as a near perfect bitch circa 1950's.

Bringing home that new puppy

Hopefully you will not bring home a wild gang like this cute bunch.

The breeder who you buy your puppy from will give you a lot of information. They will likely send you home with food as well, to get your puppy started in its new home. What you need at home ready for the puppy are the following:

Large crate. At least a 500 size crate. It will be much too large for the puppy but that will rapidly change. The puppy will find comfort and a respite from the world in his crate. Dogs love crates and if left to their choice will routinely go to it when they rest. It is not cruel, just the opposite. Of course they do not need to spend too much time crated.

Non-plastic food bowl. Plastic can be a problem. Go with stainless steal or ceramic.

Good toys to chew and teeth on. Watch for cheap toys filled with who knows what. I do not trust them and they are abundant.

A collar and leash. I am a believer in a choke collar. The soft nylon ones are great and will not break the fur very much. Choke collars are very humane when used properly, but everything should be used properly. I like the flexi leads as well. I would

A little older puppy. Even at this age you can see the utility of the head. Note how the ears are laid way back in the fur, the tight eyes with dark rims, and the tight lips again rimmed with black. Note also the clean muzzle leading to the head that is slightly domed. There is no stop on the muzzle. If you had a front view you would see the head and muzzle was also wedge shaped.

have both the standard lead and a flexi lead.

Food. See section on food. You need to feed what the breeder sent home with you or buy it. When you change food you can slowly make the change over several days by mixing the two until you have the pup on its new food without any upsets to the system.

Water bowl or bucket. Again I do not like plastic for many reasons. Also get something that will not rust. I am suspicious of galvanized pails as well.

You need to have an appointment with your Vet to check out your new puppy. Ideally that should occur within the first couple days of its arrival.

Your puppy is likely to not be so happy about being separated from its littermates. Give it time and attention, but space to rest and get the drift of its new surroundings. Within just a day or so your puppy will have moved on and embraced its new life with gusto.

Potty training can begin immediately. Pyrs are mostly very clean and generally do not like to soil where they live. Your puppy may have been paper-trained. You can train your puppy with the crate, close attention, and anticipation of its needs. Not hard at all. Puppies may have problems making it overnight, but might be able to make it pretty soon. I would start by crating and giving one potty outing during the night. This middle of the night outing should pass fairly soon. Puppies should always be put out to potty after eating or coming out of the crate. They should also be put out every couple hours in addition. Soon they may get the hang of it and be asking to go out by standing and even pawing the door to go out.

In the first day or so even with them not changing food, they may have a bit of gastric upset due to the stress of the change. Patience and gentle praise will get you past this quickly. Your puppy will want to make you happy, so play off on that.

Who could say "no" to this?

Your pet will need to follow a program of vaccinations recommended by your vet. As a guideline, most dogs at a minimum require shots covering distemper, corona, and parvovirus. At about sixteen weeks your Vet will give the final shot that will include also include leptospiria in combination with the above. He may also give the first rabies shot at this time. Your pup should have also been tested and treated for worms as well. If your pup is going to be out side consult your vet about lyme disease vaccination. My feeling is all working dogs should have this shot.

Thereafter they should be checked for worms on a periodic basis and given the appropriate management. Your Vet will also recommend checks and prevention for heartworms.

Children need to be disciplined to be very gentle with the puppy. Puppy teeth and nails are sharp. Supervise closely your

155

young children's interactions with your puppy for a long time. Soon your puppy will be big and strong and a danger to your infant and toddler in its gusto. It's your responsibility to set the ground rules and keep everyone under control for both the puppy and children's safety and well being. Don't think by one year old the puppy behavior will magically disappear. They can act like puppies intermittently for some time past one year of age. This is a long time. The rules and guidelines need to be consistent and ongoing for a good relationship with your puppy and its family members.

To me a Pyr is a true blessing given to us by God. The puppies are the future embodiment and promise of this blessing from God. Like everything else given to us by God, we have a serious responsibility to safeguard the dogs. A large part of that responsibility is understanding the breed and not placing them in impossible situations that could be abusive. They will love and protect you, your family, and your flock without question or reserve. God's expectations from you are for equal return of the care and love.

Bringing home an older Pyr

Hopefully, your older Pyr will have already passed the house breaking stage. If not, you will have to follow the steps outlined in the prior chapter.

All the prior chapter elements apply to the older dog, especially the crate. Also get to your Vet as soon as possible. Have your Vet check its teeth and schedule them to be cleaned if needed.

Not older, but who can resist a group like this? Litter at Talisman Great Pyrenees. Photo courtesy of David Dougherty.

You well. If your Pyr is a rescue Pyr, you need to give it time to adjust. It could have gone through many homes in its journey to you. It may not know for a while that this is its forever home. That is as important to your Pyr as it is important to us all.

In the older Pyr you will begin to see the full personality emerge from their guardian demeanor, that can consist of an almost stoic expression, very slowly over the next few months. You will be delighted when your Pyr loves and trusts you enough to show you its personality. That is a gift and you should recognize it as such. You will be well on your way to a special relationship like none you have ever had before. Forget the past, the dog will move on with you and give you its complete trust and love. You need to do the same in return. Give it a bit of time and space especially in the early days. Pyrs observe intently, so they will use this non-demand situation to make themselves comfortable and to figure all this out. It will also be formulating its guarding duties and determining who and what is its flock during this time.

The same vaccination schedule should apply to the adult as the puppy and of course the worm and parasite management including heartworm prevention and checks.

Pyrs generally cannot be pushed very much. They will have their own time schedule. You will likely be surprised how they will slowly evolve maybe even for as long as a year. You have to understand these are serious guarding dogs and not prone to asking favor from strangers. They seem to do this often with a stoic indifference that belies their true personality.

The Geriatric Pyr

Old Pyrs are special and wonderful animals. The grace and wisdom one sees in their eyes is beyond description. They are so calm and regal. They are still all Pyr in every way. Pyrs live to be as old as 14 or 15 years occasionally. It is not uncommon for them to live to 12 years old. Some of the problems we see in old Pyrs are what we see in many old animals i.e. arthritis, diminished eyesight, diminished hearing, and some muscle wasting. The

Madam Giralt as a child with family Pyr in Foix, France circa 1930's

Spinal Muscular degenerative disease is seen in some Pyrs at old age. This makes it more difficult for them to get up, especially after laying for a while.

Geriatric cataracts are not uncommon and give the eyes a cloudiness sometime seen with the naked eye. Sometimes their coat does not look very healthy by being dry and brittle. Many times they can be very thin.

You need to put them on a bit less protein foods so their kidneys do not have to work so hard, but do not sacrifice any quality. In fact they need the most digestible food you can get for them. Glucosomine Chondritian may be indicated to help the old joints not get too arthritic. A mild analgesic daily might make them feel a bit better if they are uncomfortable. All this under your Vets care, please. Nothing quite works as well. The GI system is less effective; all the internal organs are old as well. Teeth and gums need special attention and this is important, as gum infections are very hard on an old dog.

They can sleep harder. Their sensory system is not as keen. This can result in their not being aroused as easily from a deep sleep. Once aroused, they are quick to guard as usual. Even a very frail dog or bitch will rise up and patter around barking their hoarse, weaker bark. This a special time for them and for you as well. The love and dedication seen in them at this time is a wonderful sight and makes you appreciate the breed more than ever. The dignity, even in the face of an advanced age Pyr, is not something I believe I can quite capture in words. They are their characteristic tough self, never whining, or complaining. Sometimes taking a few tries or even needing a little boost to get up and get going, they will get going and in their minds eye be one year old again.

The hardest part is when the frail stage gets very serious. You get to the point that you start pondering the quality of life. You will resent having to ponder this unacceptable situation, but in the end they will clearly tell you when their time has come. You will know and then it's all right. They will love you all the more to lay their head in your lap as they slip gently into an eternal restful sleep.

All of us love our old ones and everyone else's as well. It's the one time in a dogs life when even the most fierce detractors of a particular show dog will soften their heart and truly be touched by the old dog going around the ring one more time, maybe for the last time. Tears abound often at these Veteran dog and bitch classes.

Food and Feeding

Top quality food is essential to us all. Your animals are no different. Unfortunately dog food companies have really let us down as an industry. There are a few exceptions. I'll not belabor this opinion too much, but give you my recommendations.

If you want to feed raw, go for it. You will find a lot of information about it in many places. I no not advise against it, but do not use it. I am a believer in human grade ingredients used in the dog's food, be that what you prepare or buy and feed. There are a few good companies out there that fit that later bill.

Madam Dretzen with a group of Pyrs circa 1911 in Paris.

I also believe strongly in a varied diet. The notion we have all been sold and many have bought into is surely from successful marketing from the dog food industry. Basically they say, get your dog on one food and never change it. They know that the food is so poor in many ways that it takes the digestive system awhile to adjust to it. So what you get is inferior, additive-laced food offered and eaten every day for years at a time. No wonder food allergies and cancer have become epidemic. Our poor dogs are captives and must eat this or starve. Pyrs have gotten by on little food historically and been able to work days upon end and be able to fight large fierce predators on little or no food, so they seem to do well on these diets. But in the end the toxic buildup will catch up with them and we do not know how long the historic dogs lived as a rule. I suspect they did not have a very long life span. So the Pyrs are left to eat the food we give them or go without basically. Also the poor quality food will go to fat quicker than the good stuff and it will take much more of the poor stuff to give any minimal level of nutrition. All this places a greater load on their system.

I recommend to you, to go to a top quality human grade dog food. Vary it as much as you can and supplement with scraps from your own food, plus trimmings, bones, hooves, and other animal byproducts that your dog can chew and eat safely. You will have to feed less, have a healthier dog and hopefully will not have allergies and if you are real lucky, not have cancer. It's not fair to blame cancer on food, as there is a heritable aspect to it seen in most large breeds, but it cannot hurt to have good healthy nutrition involved if the dog has some heritable predisposition. You certainly want those ingredients that fight against free radicals.

Look at your single protein, single carbohydrate food and vary between them. So much chicken and beef is fed that they can become a problem especially in the cheaper foods. Lamb has risen now to a problem as well. Today you can find almost anything you want, but expect to pay for it. There are no bargains in dog food. Pay for it now or pay someone else for the after effects later. There are now organic foods available and more, likely, on the way as we look to improve our dog's nutrition.

Buy Carol Brescher Boyle's great book on feeding human food. Carol has been a pioneer and is so very far ahead of her time on this subject. The book is called *Natural Food Recipes for the Healthy Dog*. You can get it online at Amazon.com or on Carols web site at http://www.naturaldogfood.com/.

Use a top quality puppy food up to 4 months old. Change to top quality dog food thereafter. Supplement food as desired, but not additives without sound professional advice. As a puppy, feed three to four small meals. By six months, two meals daily. You can continue the twice daily feeding regime thereafter, or even go to once daily if the food is left down for the dog to eat, at will during the day. If you are an advocate of "put it down for a period of time and then pick it up", continue twice daily feeding.

Diet dog food? I am not a believer. Just give a bit less of the really good quality stuff.

I am a believer in the geriatric dog food, but again make sure, especially here, it is top quality. Let's put as little load on the kidneys, etc. as we can during these wonderful old age days.

How much food will a Pyr eat? In my experience an adult will eat about 4-5 cups of food daily. Puppies when they are big and growing will eat more. I like to put it down and leave it and let them eat to satisfaction by refilling as needed during the day. Mostly they will not get fat, but watch those occasional Pyrs that will overeat and get fat. In this case you will need to measure and restrict the amount they eat.

Why such a small amount of food for such a large breed? We are told that the breed has a low metabolism. This has been bourn out by anesthesia sensitivity as well. This is one of the unique, functional aberrations of our breed, necessitated by its ancient heritage. My study of the breed tells me that the nomadic shepherds initially and then later, the various other shepherds in the Pyrenees Mountains, needed dogs who could work on little or, at times, almost no food and still have the strength and stamina to take on the predators. Those dogs that could not do this were eliminated naturally or were not used by the shepherds in their breeding. The result was those dogs that could get along without much food and still be able to wage life and death battles on behalf of the flock and shepherds, were the ones used to propagate the breed.

This is further affirmation that the breed is naturally lean, to the point of being skinny. It is a linear dog that does not waste any of its resources and that includes carrying excess weight. It's only us show people who want a heavy or even fat dog. Shame on us, but I am afraid we cannot change this now and have our dogs enjoy success in that show venue, but it's not what is natural for the breed. I am not advocating feeding less food. I am simply noting the natural tendency for the breed to be lean and not require huge amounts of food to exist in a healthy state.

General Care and Health of the Pyr

Four generations of offspring from Ch. Bonbelle du Comte de Foix lying with owner Arlene Oraby in foreground

When you visit your Vet for the first time, he or she will make sure your Pyr is current on all vaccinations. In addition they will check for worms and test for heartworms, unless your puppy is young. The Vet will give the shots you need, worm the dog or give medicine for same, recommend tick and flea control measures, and start you on heart worm preventative measures. All these are important to the happiness and long life of the Pyr.

Parvovirus

Maybe the most severe threat to your Pyr. It is important that you keep your Pyr vaccinated against this deadly disease. While some dogs with major Vet care can survive after contracting Parvo, the after effects can leave many systems of the dog damaged. The virus can live in the ground for many months. Vets report an increase in the disease after every rain.

Gastrointestinal problems that are severe, including diarrhea, bloody stools, quick loss of fluids, elevated temperature, and sometimes rapid decline resulting in death. It is highly contagious. So be careful about transporting it to your other animals on clothes, shoes, etc. Disinfect and wash everything with bleach at a minimum. Wash and spray everything that the dog touches or has come in contact   Remember if you do not kill the virus it can wait many months to be picked up by another animal.

Disinfect after the dog with bleach and clean yourself and your clothes as well. The virus can contaminate towels, hoses, floors, etc. Spray, wash, and wipe everything. Pups should be vaccinated by 16 weeks of age with a series of shots that begin about 7-8 weeks of age. Follow closely your Vets regime.

Coronavirus

Not generally as serious as Parvovirus, but can kill young, old, or sick animals. One of the fears is mutation to a more aggressive strain, so immunizations are important. It is manifest by gastrointestinal upsets mostly.

Follow the same procedure you do with Parvovirus above.

Rabies

Deadly to both humans and animals. The best and really only defense is vaccination. Pups should be vaccinated by 12-15 weeks. Follow your Vets procedure for vaccinations.

Distemper

Distemper is an old viral disease that was the scourge of dogs prior to the development of a vaccine. It is a killer and few dogs survive. It affects the nervous system causing seizures and other severe problems. Follow Vets protocol for vaccinations, as prevention is the only real remedy. If you see it or come in contact with it, best to follow the procedure you would with Parvovirus.

Bordetella

Also known as Kennel Cough, it can make your dog sick, but generally is not a killer. It can kill young, sick, or old animals.

The disease is respiratory and pulmonary. It can lead to more severe problems. It is very contagious and is airborne. If you travel and take your dog along with you frequently, attend any type dog activity, or board your dog (even going to the vet can be hazardous) it is best to vaccinate. Treatment can be expensive and the dog can be slow to respond.

Canine Hepatitis

It can damage your dog's liver and can result in death. This type of hepatitis is presently not transferable to humans. It is controlled by vaccine usually in a combination shot that gets parvovirus, corona virus, distemper, and sometimes Leptospirosis (four forms).

Leptospirosis

Leptospirosis is a bacterial disease that affects humans and animals. It is caused by bacteria. There are many different strains (serovars). Of these different strains there are eight that are of importance for dogs. Right now only four of the strains are covered in vaccinations, so the dog is at risk for the others. It causes a wide range of symptoms, and some infected may have no symptoms at all. Symptoms of leptospirosis include high fever, severe headache, chills, muscle aches, and vomiting, and may include jaundice (yellow skin and eyes), red eyes, abdominal pain, diarrhea, or a rash. If the disease is not treated, the patient could develop kidney damage, meningitis (inflammation of the membrane around the brain and spinal cord), liver failure, and respiratory distress. In rare cases death occurs. Again young, sick, or old animals are most at risk.

Normally the vaccine for this is not given until the last shot or shots in the series of shots done in the combination manner. It can cause a vaccine reaction because of the type vaccine that is employed.

Lyme Disease

If your dog is outside a great deal, you need to consult with your vet on this very serious disease. Various ticks from the genus Ixodes are the carriers of this nasty disease, mostly determined by what part of the country you live. This is a potentially serious disease with several manifestations, both acute and chronic. Both the hard bodied adult and larvae stage of the tick spread it. It can

Ixades Scapularis or Deer Tick seen primarily in eastern North America

be difficult to diagnose and is done mostly via clinical picture and exposure potential. The "rash" is diagnostic, but is not always seen.

Symptoms are meningoencephalitis, cardiac

171

inflammation, and arthritis, but it can attack many places in acute or chronic symptoms, both very mild to quite severe. Treatment is antibiotics. Sometimes multiple trials and sometimes long term administration of the antibiotics is required. It can be difficult to treat and animals can have a residual that lingers on, sometimes on and off in symptoms.

In the past vaccines have not been very effective, but there is hope that newer ones are more effective. The best handling is prevention, but this is near impossible for dogs working in the field.

Grooming your Great Pyrenees

As we discussed earlier, if you can get a dog with the proper dry flat coat the job will be much easier. Some show breeders want that huge even wiry coat, but it can be a disaster when they work. In your home as a pet, the proper coat is much easier to keep nice than the other coat. If I had to get two grooming tools, one would

Undercoat rake

be a long tooth rake (undercoat rake) and the other would be comfortable in my hand comb. The long tooth rake will get into the undercoat and help loosen and remove the soft wooly coat that all the dogs have in winter. The comb will let you demat and comb the rest of the coat. If your Pyr gets hard mats, you will need a mat splitter or a lot of patience and a dog that is very tolerant.

I recommend the following tools for grooming:

Long tooth rake

Comb

Mat splitter

Scissors (shears)

Thinning scissors

Nail clipper

The list above is a good normal list for most of us. The scissors you will use to trim out small mats and take excess hair from feet. The thinning scissors will likewise be helpful for mats and just taking out some areas of

Nail clippers, scissor type

profuse hair by thinning. The mat splitter is self-explanatory. Some of these mats are very tough. The nail trimmer should be the scissor type that lets you get around the nail by opening up the scissor action. Sometimes the dewclaws grow around making a full circle and the closed end clipper,

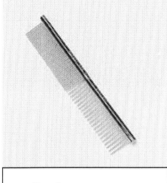

Comb

guillotine type, cannot get around the nail to trim it. These dewclaws, frequently in some dogs, can grow into the pad they grow from and become quite painful.

Very little grooming occurs in the working environments, but in your home it's different. The dewclaws

Mat splitter tool

are an exception that needs attention to at least every few months even when working. Pyrs need few baths really. The dry coast is truly self-shedding of the dirt and debris. Get the mats and tangles out before the bath. After the bath the wet will tighten the mats and tangles and be a good place for bacterial infections to grow that result in "hot spots." Use a good dog shampoo. When bathing your Pyr, it is important that you rinse the soap completely from the skin. The skin of a Pyr is their true weak link and any residual soap left behind will likely start a skin irritation that will lead to hot spots. Hot spots are bacterial infections of the skin that requires antibiotics, shaving the area, and astringents to dry the skin. Dogs working in heat, if it's humid, are much more prone to

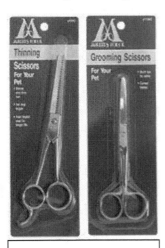

this. So rinse till you see no evidence of soap in the water and maybe even consider a vinegar rinse. I would mix four ounces of white (clear) vinegar to a quart of water. It will cut any residual soap on the skin and help change the pH also, which will be a plus.

Two types of scissors

Penny Lane gets her first bath. Shown with owner Lisa Taylor.

Towel dry or better, blow-dry if you have a blower. Ideally you do not want so much heat with the blower as you do forced air. If you towel well and the dog shakes vigorously, they will get the job done. Keep them out of the dirt and/or debris until completely dry

Resources

The breeder where you got your Pyr is always your best resource. After that, the Great Pyrenees Club of America and the American Kennel Club should be able to help you with many questions.

Great Pyrenees Club of America

This club has addresses that potentially change from time to time. They can always be reached through the AKC and presently their web site is part of AKC's web site. The URL for the club at the present time is:

http://clubs.akc.org/gpca/

American Kennel Club

The mailing address for the AKC is

AKC Operations Center
5580 Centerview Drive
Raleigh, NC 27606
http://akc.org

The Great Pyrenees Owner's Handbook pays tribute to one of the special creatures in God's creation. I am indebted to all the legions of owners who preceded me. I must thank my family who shared the love and care of these dogs these past thirty plus years. Maryann, my dear and lovely wife, who has traveled this road with me every step of the way, has aided me more than she will ever know and made the journey ever so pleasant. I have been inspired by the love, dedication, and great sacrifices that those that came before us gave so freely and willingly on behalf of the breed.

To all my friends who have loved the breed along with me, I thank you.

Joe Gentzel

Front Cover:

Champion Aneto Leornardo de Puppius Maximus, owned by Lee and Janet Hancock.

Back Cover:

From left to right, Champion Tip'N Chip Mustang Sally owned by Joe and Maryann Gentzel and the Best in Show Champion Whitehope Pneuma owned by David and Dale Dougherty of Talisman Great Pyrenees

and

the famous painting by Jean-Baptiste Oudry, titled; *Chasse aux Loups*, circa in 1746.